A Bonus Offer!

To thank you for buying this copy of *Vogue Sewing for the Home,* Vogue Patterns would like to offer you a Vogue Pattern of your choice at a special price. Fill out the appropriate coupon below or on the next page and send it to the address specified. Include payment by check or money order, not cash please, and allow 2 to 4 weeks for delivery.

Vogue Patterns

✂ --

In the **UNITED STATES** send to: Vogue Pattern Services
P.O. Box 549
Altoona, PA 16603

Offer: any Vogue Pattern for $3.00 (plus $.50 postage and handling)

special offer	$3.00
postage/handling	.50
total enclosed	$3.50

Please send pattern no. _____ in size _____ to:

Name _____

Address _____

City _____ State _____ Zip Code _____

✂ --

In **CANADA** send to: Butterick Canada, Inc.
P.O. Box 4001 Station A
Toronto, Ontario
M5W 1H9

Offer: $4.00 OFF the regular price of any Vogue Pattern (plus $.75 postage and handling)

regular price	_____
special offer	− $4.00
sub total	_____
postage/handling	+ $ .75
total enclosed	_____

Please send pattern no. _____ in size _____ to:

Name _____

Address _____

City _____

Province _____

Postal Code _____

Offer not valid on pattern nos. 1001 and 1002

In the **UNITED KINGDOM** send to: Vogue Pattern Service
New Lane,
Hants P09 2ND
England

Offer: one-half regular retail price of any Vogue Pattern (plus postage and handling of 25p in the UK and 45p elsewhere)

regular price _____
minus ½ regular price _____
subtotal _____
plus postage/handling _____ (25p in the UK; 45p elsewhere)
total enclosed _____

Please send pattern no. _____ in size _____ to:
[block letters please]

Name _____

Street _____

Town _____

County _____

Postal Code _____

Country _____

Offer not valid on pattern nos. 1001 and 1002

✂ --

In **AUSTRALIA** send to: Butterick Company PTY. LTD.
1 Queen Street
Auburn NSW 2144
Australia

In **NEW ZEALAND** send to: Butterick (N.Z.) Limited
34–38 Kalmia Street
Ellerslie
Auckland 5
New Zealand

Offer: $3.00 OFF the regular price of any Vogue Pattern (plus $.50 for postage and handling)

regular price _____
special offer − $3.00
sub total _____
postage/handling + $ .50
total enclosed _____

Please send pattern no. _____ in size _____ to:

Name _____

Address _____

City/Postal Code _____

Country _____

Offer not valid on pattern nos. 1001 and 1002

VOGUE
SEWING FOR THE HOME

PERENNIAL LIBRARY

HARPER & ROW, PUBLISHERS, NEW YORK

Cambridge, Philadelphia, San Francisco, Washington
London, Mexico City, São Paulo, Singapore, Sydney

Writer: *Peggy Bendel*

Illustrator: *Phoebe Adams Gaughan*

Editor: *Helen Moore*

Coordinator for Butterick: *Patricia Perry*

Butterick staff: *Jane Glanzer, Carol Sharma, Renee Ullman, Ron Ferguson*

Coordinator for Harper & Row: *Carol Cohen*

Harper & Row production staff: *Leta Evanthes, Lydia Link, Coral Tysliava, Diane Conley*

A hardcover edition of this book is published by Harper & Row, Publishers, Inc.

VOGUE SEWING FOR THE HOME. Copyright © 1986 by Butterick Company, Inc. All rights reserved. Printed in the United States of America. No part of this book may be used or reproduced in any manner whatsoever without written permission except in the case of brief quotations embodied in critical articles and reviews. For information address Harper & Row, Publishers, Inc., 10 East 53rd Street, New York, N.Y. 10022. Published simultaneously in Canada by Fitzhenry & Whiteside Limited, Toronto.

First PERENNIAL LIBRARY edition published 1987

Designed by Jos. Trautwein/Bentwood Studio

Library of Congress Cataloging-in-Publication Data
Main entry under title:

Vogue sewing for the home.

 "Perennial Library."
 Includes index.
 Contributions by Butterick Company, Inc.
 1. Sewing.   2. House furnishings.   I. Butterick Company.
TT715.V64   1987   646.2′1   85-45033
ISBN 0-06-091409-2 (pbk.)

87 88 89 90 91 FG 10 9 8 7 6 5 4 3 2 1

Other books from Vogue

Contents

How to Use This Book

Vogue Sewing for the Home is designed to help you take the shortest route from decorating idea to decorating reality. The first section, Getting Started, is a shopping guide for fabrics and other materials, tools, supplies, and equipment. It tells you what to purchase, where to find it, and how to make a wise selection.

Sewing Techniques comes next. It's in alphabetical order for convenient reference, and presents a repertoire of sewing techniques for working on home decorating projects. The emphasis is on using your sewing machine to the utmost advantage, and exploring ways you can use it to take shortcuts.

Then there's a series of project portfolios: Window Treatments, Bed Treatments, Pillows, and Table Coverings and Accessories. Complete how-to information is given so you can duplicate the projects of your choice, or better yet, use them to spark your own ideas. In each category, the basic construction method is given first so you can see how easy it is to spin off many stylish, one-of-a-kind variations. The dressmaker's custom of using ⅝″ (15mm) seam allowances is followed throughout, unless stated otherwise at the start of the project instructions, so there's no need to learn new sewing habits. Whenever you come across a sewing term in SMALL CAPITAL LETTERS, this is your clue to refer to the Sewing Techniques section. The information given there teaches new skills to beginning home sewers and reacquaints more experienced sewers with skills not often used.

Finally, there's a Resource Directory. It includes manufacturers who can direct you to local shops that stock the fabrics, trimmings, and other materials needed for your decorating projects. There are also mail order sources for various kinds of supplies and fabric services, so regardless of where you live you can sew beautiful, soft furnishings for the place you call home.

Getting Started

You'll find sewing for your home is creative, rewarding, and surprisingly easy. This is true whether you're decorating on a budget or can spend freely, whether you're planning a total makeover or just want to freshen up an existing room with a few new items, and whether you live in a studio apartment or the quintessential mansion.

Surely, sewing for your home is a special kind of sewing. Most of the time your pattern is a set of measurements. You use them to mark off cutting lines for simple, straight fabric panels. These panels are then finished with various seams, hems, and headings to make curtains, shades, coverlets, pillows, table coverings, and other fabric furnishings to decorate your home.

For several reasons, sewing this way is easier than dressmaking. In decorating projects, 99 percent of the sewing is machine stitching, so there's little handwork to fuss over. You have the option of using quick fusing methods in many situations. Perhaps best of all, there are no fitting headaches—it's much easier to fit curtains on a rectangular window than to fit a skirt or blouse to the contours of the female torso!

Probably some of the fabrics and supplies you'll use to sew for your home will seem like old friends. Some of the tools and equipment may seem familiar too, but there's a whole world of specialty findings and fixings which belong solely to the "home furnishings" category.

It's a world worth exploring, for in it is everything you need to create projects which are, in the finest sense, custom made. There are also items which save you precious sewing time as well. Shopping for them takes you beyond general fabric stores and into the lumberyard, craft and hobby shop, hardware store, outlets specializing in drapery and upholstery supplies, as well as home improvement centers.

Fabrics

Many home decorating projects begin when you find a beautiful fabric, and this is an excellent starting point. Above all, choose a fabric you love: when you express your taste, you stamp your personality on a room. But you should also think about how the fabric contributes mood and style, and if it's practical for day-to-day living.

MOOD AND STYLE

If you're planning a large project such as curtains, a bedspread, or a mass of toss pillows in assorted textures, your choice of fabric sets the mood and establishes a decorating theme for the entire room. The list of popular home decorating fabrics beginning on page 17 is a good source of ideas. For a formal feeling, there are velvet, satin, lace, and tone-on-tone jacquard weaves that are the glory of the weaver's art. No less elegant although more understated are crisp linen weaves, synthetic suedes, and luxurious raw silks. In a cozy, put-your-feet-up frame of mind are easy-care, casual fabrics such as gingham, corduroy, and homespun. If you prefer a sleek, contemporary ambiance, you might use wool flannel or natural canvas to create an inviting atmosphere.

Printed fabrics can add instant style and interest to a room, and there's a wide selection available for sewing—historical reproductions, smart grids, romantic florals, country modern mini-prints, exotic batiks, and whimsical nursery motifs, to name a few. Combining several prints in a room gives a custom-designed look to your sewing, and many manufacturers offer coordinated fabric groups to make this a foolproof proposition. Another no-fail option: fabrics printed to match wallpapers can be ordered from many sources.

IS IT PRACTICAL?

Although a fabric's beauty is your first consideration, you should make sure it's also a practical choice. If you're making curtains, you'll want a fabric which won't fade readily. Although all colors fade as time goes by, blues and deep, rich colors fade sooner than others. If you're covering chair cushions, you'll want a fabric that is strong and long-wearing, so it's best to select fabric with a tight, even weave.

Look on the fabric label to see what kind of care is required. Can you machine-wash it, or does it need dry-cleaning? Items for a child's room should be easy to care for, as should tablecloths and placemats and other items which are used daily for family living. Something to keep in mind: plain fabrics show soil more easily than prints or textured weaves, and light or very dark colors look soiled and dusty faster than midrange colors.

It's a definite plus if large, detailed projects such as ruffled curtains or layered bed ensembles can be washed and dried without tedious hand-pressing afterward. A toss pillow, on the other hand, is made to lend a spot of color or texture. It's ornamental rather than functional, so it's one of the rare home decorating items which can be sewn from a delicate fabric.

Fibers Whether or not a fabric lives up to your expectations depends to a great extent upon the fibers it's made from. Check the label on the bolt to find out a fabric's fiber content. Usually this is a blend of two or more different fibers.

Many people think fiber and fabric mean the same, but they are distinctly different. Fiber is the basic material from which a fabric is made. Every fabric has a generic name which refers pri-

marily to the way the cloth is woven. A fiber such as cotton may be woven into many different generic fabrics—flannel, broadcloth, velveteen, or chintz, for example. Even though the fiber is the same, the fabric is quite different in each case. Calling any of these fabrics "cotton" wouldn't define the type of fabric, or tell you what the fabric looks like. It would tell you only what fiber was used to make the fabric.

It's important to know which fiber recipe was used to make a fabric because fibers have so much to do with a fabric's practical performance. Some fibers are easily dyed, but others are not and the colors will fade or run, for example. Study the chart of fibers below—it's a good shopping guide because it lists the plusses and minuses inherent to a fabric by fiber content. If your fabric is a blend of fibers, it's been engineered to emphasize each fiber's advantages and minimize the disadvantages.

Bring Home a Sample First

If you're buying fabric for a major project, ask the store for a large sample or buy ½ yd (0.50m) to bring home. At home:

- See how the colors look under your lighting. Test this with natural daylight, and at night with the lamps turned on.

- Check if the color, texture, mood, and style of the fabric blend well with the furnishings in the room.

- If it's a print, study it from across the room. This is how you'll live with it, and many prints "read" differently from a distance than up close. For example, mini-prints can look like solids from across the room unless the print motif contrasts boldly with the background color.

- Crush the fabric to see how easily it wrinkles.

- Hold it up to the light to check if the weave is tight and firm, a mark of quality for all but sheer, open-weave fabrics.

- If the fabric's for a window treatment, pin it up at the window to see how it looks when sunlight filters through. Test how it looks and drapes when arranged into soft folds.

- Save your sample and use it to test for shrinkage before cutting out project sections. Use it to try out pressing and sewing techniques, too.

Shopping Guide for Fibers

FIBER	BIGGEST VIRTUES	MAJOR DRAWBACKS
Acetate	Silken luster Drapes well Resists moths, mildew	Atmospheric fumes will fade colors unless vat-dyed or solution-dyed Weakened by sunlight
Acrylic	Warm for its weight Dyes well Resists moths, mildew, sun damage Easy care	Is weak when wet Tends to pill Accumulates static electricity
Cotton	Strong even when wet Absorbent Dyes well	Shrinks Wrinkles Damaged by mildew, sun
Glass	Strong Rich texture Resists heat, flame, sun damage, wrinkles Easy care	Fibers break—slivers can injure hands and contaminate tub used for washing fabric
Linen	Strong Rich texture Crisp body	Dyes well only in "natural" colors—others may run or fade Shrinks Wrinkles
Metallic	Decorative gleam	Melts easily
Modacrylic	Lustrous Resists flame	Very sensitive to heat

Nylon	Very strong	Sun fades colors
	Lustrous	May pill
	Resists soil, wrinkles, moths, mildew	
Olefin	Strong	Difficult to dye
	Fast drying	Sensitive to heat
	Resists soil, mildew, weather damage	
Polyester	Strong	Hard to remove stains
	Resists wrinkles, shrinking, mildew, moths, sun damage	Accumulates static electricity
	Easy care	
Rayon	Soft	Weak when wet
	Dyes well	Damaged by sun
		Shrinks
		Stretches out of shape
Silk	Lustrous	Weakened by sunlight
	Strong	Colors may run or change after cleaning
	Resists moths, mildew	May water spot
Wool	Resilient	Shrinks
	Warm	Attracts moths
	Dyes well	
	Durable	
Vinyl	Waterproof	Sensitive to heat—softens at low temperatures
	Wipes clean	

Finishes and Other Processes
Special finishes can improve the way fibers perform, and certain manufacturing processes can add bonus qualities to your fabric. Look on the label to see if your fabric has one or more of these extras:

- Colorfast—the color won't wash out or fade upon exposure to sunlight and other atmospheric elements.

- Flame retardant—the fabric discourages the spreading of flames, either because the fibers used have this quality or because a chemical finish has been applied to the fabric.

- Mildew resistant—resists the growth of mildew and other molds.

- Mothproof—repels moths.

- Permanent press or durable press—you can wash and dry the fabric by machine; it sheds wrinkles without requiring ironing.

- Preshrunk—the fabric has undergone preliminary preshrinking; the percentage of residual shrinkage must be declared on the label.

- Soil release—dirt and oil stains can be removed easily because soil won't penetrate the fibers.

- Solution-dyed—the fibers were dyed before the fabric was woven; these dyes are long-lasting.

- Stain resistant—repels soil and stains and prevents them from sinking beneath the fabric surface.

- Vat-dyed—a type of dye that creates colors more likely to withstand laundering.

- Vinylized—chemically coated to make the fabric wipe-clean and waterproof.

- Wash-and-wear, easy care, or minimum care—the fabric can be washed and requires little or no ironing to remove wrinkles.

- Waterproof—the fabric is, or has been made, nonporous so water will not penetrate.

- Wrinkle or crease resistant—resists and recovers from wrinkling.

Finishes You Can Do Yourself
Certain key fabric finishes can be applied at home or sent out for a professional treatment. To repel stains, you can buy spray cans of fabric protector under brand names such as Zepel® and Scotchguard®, or your local dry cleaner might offer this service as well as others, such as water-repellent finishes and steam-pressing for preshrinking. Fabrics can be vinylized on a mail-order basis; for a complete list of resources, see page 187.

Cost Though quality fabrics can be costly, they tend to last longer and look better—factors which make them bargains in the long run. However, if your budget is tight, there are ways to use inexpensive fabrics which won't look like you've been counting pennies. It's better to select a discount fabric and use it lavishly for curtains, for example, than to use a more expensive fabric and skimp on the fullness. Bed sheets can be an economical source of fabric, especially if you can find the ones you like on sale and their light weight suits your project

without the extra expense of quilting them or adding a lining.

Some types of projects use more fabric than others, something to consider right from the beginning. Flat roller shades, for example, use little fabric compared to the shirred fullness of balloon shades. Layered bed ensembles with coverlet, pillow shams, and a separate dust ruffle take more fabric than a plain throw bedspread which covers all in one layer; the same point is true for multilayered window and table treatments.

If you select a plaid, striped, or printed fabric, your costs might be greater than if you use a solid color if extra fabric is needed to balance the design and match it at the seams. If you're planning ruffles, covered cord welting, or bias-bound edges, you'll need extra fabric too. However, these custom trimmings can save you a considerable amount of money compared to the cost of buying ready-made trims.

While fabric may be the single largest expense in a project, it's not the only one. Add up the costs for all the other supplies (such as tapes, linings, pillow forms, and curtain rods) needed to sew and install a project to arrive at a realistic estimate of the cost. If your fabric must be dry-cleaned, this is another expense to think about.

Also figure in your time, surely a valuable commodity. Compare how long it will take you to complete a project with how long you expect to live with it. Decorating a weekend home or a temporary rental apartment suggests using low-cost supplies for quick, easy projects. But if you're making a bassinet ensemble to hand down for generations, or decorating the living room of the permanent family homestead, naturally it makes sense to invest in prime materials and put your time into details and fine workmanship.

One last practical factor: compare the cost of sewing your own home decorating items to the cost of buying them or having them made on a special-order basis. Sometimes it's better to buy—a pillow form isn't much of a bargain to make, unless you need an odd size or shape, for example. Most times, however, you'll save so much by sewing a project for your home that you'll feel justified if you splurge on a gorgeous fabric or an exquisite trim.

TYPES OF HOME DECORATING FABRICS

The following types of fabrics are popular and frequently recommended for sewing for the home.

Batiste—a sheer, fine, lightweight fabric; drapes softly. Very lightweight batiste is woven from cotton/polyester fibers.

Broadcloth—a smooth, tightly woven, lightweight or medium-weight fabric; usually all-cotton or an easy-care cotton/polyester blend.

Canvas—a heavy, strong, plain-weave fabric made from linen or cotton fibers, or blends of these and other fibers. Canvas is heavier than duck or sailcloth, although similar to both.

Casement cloth—a general name for a loose, open-weave fabric made for window treatments; distinctive because of the interesting textures and sheer, light-filtering quality. Casement cloths have a tendency to shrink and sag with changes in temperature and humidity.

Chenille—a fabric with tufts arranged in a decorative pattern on the right side; often used for bedspreads.

Chintz—a closely woven fabric with a shiny glaze on the right side; crisp, stiff finish. Chintz is usually all-cotton or a cotton blend, and comes in floral prints as well as solid colors. Poor grades of chintz loose their sheen quickly and tend to tear.

Corduroy—a plush, durable fabric, usually with ribs called wales on the right side; often an easy-care cotton/polyester blend. There are many weights, from superfine and lightweight baby wale to heavy, thick, bulky jumbo wale. Corduroy tends to ravel.

Damask—a woven, raised, shiny design usually of flowers or figures which are arranged as a border on a matte background; it's a type of jacquard weave. Traditional for fine tablecloths and napkins, damask may be cotton, linen, or a blend of fibers. Most damasks are reversible.

Dotted Swiss—a fine, sheer fabric with woven or printed opaque dots. The dots may also be flocked (printed in a raised texture).

Duck—a durable, plain-weave fabric which is lighter in weight

Look Closely Before You Buy

Inspect a fabric closely before you buy it. Fabrics can rarely be returned without incurring a financial penalty. Check to be sure that:

- The fabric is on-grain. The crosswise and lengthwise threads should crisscross at right angles and look straight, not wavy or pulled to one side or the other. Prints must be printed straight on the grain, both across the fabric and lengthwise. Reject any off-grain fabrics, no matter how attractively priced, because they'll always look and hang askew.

- The color is uniform. Inspect the fabric opened up flat so you can spot any distortions. Buy all the fabric you need from a single bolt, because colors can vary otherwise. If you need more than one bolt's worth to sew multiple projects for a room, buy the fabric for each project from separate bolts. For example, buy fabric for the bedspread from one bolt, and the fabric for a matching bedside table covering from another. Variations in color shading are less apparent this way.

17

than canvas, but often called canvas.

Eyelet—a smooth, plain-weave fabric such as batiste or broadcloth which is embroidered with open designs; it's sometimes called eyelet lace. Available with either an all-over embroidered design, or a border along one lengthwise edge, eyelet is also available in narrow widths as trims.

Flannel—a soft fabric with a brushed surface. It's usually made of cotton, a cotton blend, or wool fibers.

Flannelette—a lightweight version of flannel, which is often available in children's prints.

Fleece—a deep, thick, soft fabric woven from wool or acrylic fibers and resembling a blanket.

Gingham—a lightweight, plain-weave fabric with woven checks, usually made from cotton or a cotton blend. Lesser qualities of gingham have printed checks.

Homespun—a fairly loose-woven fabric made from uneven yarns for a texture which looks handmade.

Jacquard—a type of weave with a tone-on-tone design, often a shiny motif on a matte background and intricate in design. Damask is a type of jacquard weave. Some jacquard weave fabrics are reversible.

Lace—a sheer, open fabric with a net background; lace has no grainline and does not ravel. Silk lace is very fine, fragile, and lightweight. Cotton or acrylic lace is heavier and thicker. Polyester or nylon laces are very sheer and lightweight, and can be cared for easily; these laces are often manufactured with finished selvages for use as curtain panels.

Linen weaves—the term "linen" is often used to describe any fabric which has the slubbed texture and crisp finish of fabrics woven from true linen fibers. Linen-type fabrics are made from 100 percent linen, linen/cotton, and cotton/polyester blends, among others. The more linen fiber in the fabric, the more prone it is to wrinkling. Linen weaves come in many weights. *Handkerchief linen*, sometimes called cambric, is the finest, lightest version and qualifies as a semi-sheer fabric. In general, linen weaves are not tightly and firmly woven, and the fabric is likely to ravel.

Moiré—a fabric with a wavy, rippling design like watermarks; it has a sheen. If made from acetate fiber, the design is permament; if made from other fibers, the design is not.

Muslin—has a plain weave and is usually woven from cotton or cotton/polyester fibers. Weights range from sheer to heavy. Unbleached muslin is an off-white color; bleached muslin is white. Lightweight muslin is inexpensive and often used as a lining fabric.

Ninon—a transparent, mesh fabric usually made of nylon or polyester and used for curtains.

Organdy—a sheer, lightweight fabric with a stiff finish; it's usually woven from polyester and is popular for curtains. Cotton organdy wrinkles easily and loses its crispness.

Piqué—is woven with small, raised geometric patterns; it's usually crisp and medium-weight. Most piqués are easy-care cotton/polyester blends, although some are all-cotton.

Raw silk—a luxury fabric which is woven from silk fibers before they have been processed; the nubby, distinctive texture drapes stiffly.

Sailcloth—lighter than canvas, but heavier than duck. It's often used for cushion covers, tailored bedspreads, and fabric shades.

Sateen—a strong, lustrous fabric made of cotton or a cotton blend. It's often printed in stripes and bright solid colors for home furnishing fabrics.

Satin—a type of weave which creates a shiny surface on the right side of the fabric. It's slippery to handle. *Antique satin* is a popular home furnishing fabric that can be used on either side; one side is smooth and shiny, while the other side has a slight sheen and a slubbed texture.

Sheeting—a strong, lightweight, woven fabric available in great widths by the yard (meter), or as bed sheets. It's usually cotton/polyester or all-cotton. *Percale* is a type of sheeting with many threads per square inch (2.5cm); its tight, firm weave makes it especially durable.

Synthetic suede—a luxury fabric which won't ravel and has no grainline, but has a brushed surface with a definite direction in terms of color shading; it's easy to care for. Lightweight synthetic suedes such as Lamous® and Facile™ require no special sewing techniques, but heavy weights such as Ultrasuede® may require special sewing techniques similar to those used for real leather.

Taffeta—a shiny, smooth fabric made from fibers such as rayon, acetate, or silk which have a natural luster. Taffeta is usually crisp, and may be stiff.

Velvet—a fabric with a short, closely woven, plush texture on the right side; velvet ravels, and is easily damaged by steam. Silk and rayon velvets are delicate; cotton velvet is strong and long-wearing.

Velveteen—a fabric similar to velvet, but usually woven from cotton or cotton/polyester fibers.

Voile—a lightweight, sheer, crisp fabric popular for curtains; woven from easy-care cotton blends.

Does Your Fabric Need Special Handling?

Many of the popular home decorating fabrics require some sort of special attention. At times, but not always, this means buying more fabric or taking the time for extra construction steps:

- Fabrics with a soft or shiny surface need "with-nap" cutting plans. Plaids, stripes, and prints may require extra fabric as well as special cutting plans (see CUTTING LAYOUTS, page 39).

- Sheers, including lace, need special seams and hems. Synthetic suede and vinyl do, too (see FABRICS THAT REQUIRE SPECIAL HANDLING, page 41).

- Fabrics which ravel should have all their raw edges finished, and the seams should be self-finishing types which enclose the raw edges (see SEAMS, page 62).

Trims

Adding trims is an easy way to convey an impression of fine detailing, and there are many creative options. Trims can be inserted in seams for decorative accents, or applied on or near a finished edge such as a hem to form a beautiful border. If you're trimming one project in a room, it's a good idea to repeat the trim somewhere else in the setting for a unified look.

SELECTING TRIMS

There are many kinds of trims to consider, from tailored cordings to magnificent swagged fringes and wide lace edgings. Representative types of trims are described below. Laces, ribbons, bias tapes, and bias bindings are most likely to be found where dressmaking supplies are sold. Shop for home furnishing trims such as braid, cording, fringe, and tassels in stores specializing in drapery and upholstery supplies.

Bring along a large fabric sample when selecting trims so you can see how all the colors and textures blend. A contrast in both color and texture between trim and fabric is often more effective than striving for a perfect match. Check the care requirements of the trim to be sure they're compatible with those of your fabric. Many home furnishing trims require dry cleaning; trims sold for dressmaking are more likely to be washable.

If you're trimming a major project such as curtains or bedspreads, bring a sample of the trim home before you buy. Test how well the colors coordinate in the room's lighting, and step a room's length away to see if the trim looks in scale. An easy mistake to make is selecting a trim which is too delicate or too narrow to make an impact. Combining several trims is one way professional decorators solve this problem—a way to create a one-of-a-kind look, too.

TYPES OF TRIMS

Bias Bindings—precut from solid or printed polyester/cotton broadcloth, bias bindings are used to encase raw edges. The bias cut makes the binding pliant for a smooth finish whether project edges are curved or straight. Bias binding is double-fold, which means the raw edges have been pressed under, then the binding has been pressed in half; this is the ready-to-sew form for encasing edges. The standard prepackaged width is ¼" (6mm) wide, extra-wide bias binding is ½" (13mm) wide, and quilt binding is ⅞" (22mm) wide; 1" (2.5cm) binding is also available by the yard. You can also make custom bias bindings (see BIAS TAPES AND BINDINGS).

Bias Tapes—these are like bias bindings except that they are single-fold and only the raw edges have been pressed under. Three precut widths are available—½", ⅞", and 2" (13mm, 22mm, and 5cm). Any can be topstitched as a band trim, and the widest tape is often used as a hem facing. You can also make your own bias tapes (see BIAS TAPES AND BINDINGS).

Braids—flat braid with two finished edges may be knitted, woven, or plaited. Choose a flexible braid to trim a curved edge, and a firmly woven braid for loops on tab-top curtains. *Gimp* is a type of braid with small scallops of fine cord along the edges; originally used to cover upholstery tacks, it's often used now as a band trim.

Cording—the general name for round edgings. *Welting* is cord covered with bias-cut fabric strips. Ready-made weltings usually have ⅛″ or ¼″ (3 or 6mm) cord as the filler, and a durable fabric in a solid color as the covering. These weltings have a ½″ (13mm) seam allowance so the welting can be inserted in a seam; welting insertions make seams stronger as well as trim them. Soft *piping cord* is available without a fabric covering so you can make custom welting for a project (see WELTING); diameters range from very fine ⅛″ (3mm) to jumbo 1″ (2.5cm). *Cable cord*, which is a firmer, twisted cord, is available in very fine ¹⁄₁₆″ (2mm) and medium ⅜″ (10mm) diameters for the same purpose.

Eyelet—many kinds and widths are available, but the choice of colors for this embroidered cloth trim is usually limited to white or ecru. *Eyelet beading* has ladderlike slits through which ribbon can be threaded. *Eyelet edging* has one decorative, finished border, and one raw edge which is scalloped; the raw edge must be trimmed straight across before application. *Flat eyelet trim* has both long edges finished in a decorative border design, and can be topstitched like a band trim. *Ruffled eyelet* is edging which is gathered along the raw edge, then finished with a lightweight binding.

Fabric borders—printed, lightweight, all-cotton fabric borders from ⅝″ to 3⅛″ (15mm to 7.9cm) wide are available to match and coordinate with many fabrics. The long edges of these borders are raw and require finishing. Fold under the raw edges to use the border as a band trim, stitch them into seams as insertions, or hem one edge and gather the other to use as a ruffle.

Fringe—is an edge trim made of hanging yarns or cords that are knotted, braided, or stitched together along the top. The fringes suitable for projects such as fabric window treatments are heavier and more elaborate than those typically used in dressmaking. *Knotted fringe* is often made of cotton fibers and has several rows of knots in a decorative pattern at the heading; the ends of this fringe look like tassels. In a *looped fringe*, the ends are uncut. *Moss fringe* is a narrow, thick trim made from wool or acrylic fibers so the fringe is fluffy. *Pompon fringe* has a narrow braid heading with round pompons dangling at frequent intervals. *Swag fringe* has a straight heading with a scalloped edge; there may be individual tassels hanging from the scallop points.

Lace—many types of lace trims are available, from very sheer, fine net background laces to heavier crocheted laces. *Lace edging* has one decorative scalloped border, and one straight edge. *Galloon lace* is similar to flat eyelet trim because both long edges are finished with a decorative border design. *Ruffled lace* is an edging which is gathered, then finished with a net binding; similar lace trims come prepleated.

Ribbon—ribbons are available in widths from ¹⁄₁₆″ (2mm) to several inches (cm), and are a dainty trim. Usually, ribbons are combined with other trims such as lace or eyelet beading for home decorating projects. While ribbons look delicate, those made from polyester or nylon fibers are very durable and easy to launder. *Grosgrain* ribbon has fine ribs and a subtle sheen which gives it a crisp, tailored look. *Satin* and *velvet* ribbons look like their fabric namesakes. There are plaid, striped, and embroidered ribbons, as well as novelty ribbons printed with cartoon characters or nursery motifs for children's items.

Tassels—several strands of yarn or cord bound together near the top to form a pendant ornament. They are sold individually for the corners of pillows, decorative shade pulls, or as accents for window swags. Heavy rayon or cotton cord tiebacks with bell-shaped tassels are often used for floor-length curtains. *Chainette tassels* are made from a fine-twist yarn, *bullion tassels* from a heavy twisted cord, and *pompon tassels* from fluffy cotton yarn.

Tools and Equipment

The right tools and equipment help you do a professional job when sewing for your home. The items described here are useful for most decorating projects. Additional equipment specifically for window treatments is described beginning on page 81, and at the start of each project category for your use as a shopping guide.

MEASURING

It's essential to have a rigid ruler for measuring flat surfaces such as tabletops and window openings, and a flexible tape to measure soft or contoured surfaces such as pillow forms and beds. You'll find these measuring tools very practical:

- Folding ruler—rigid metal or wood, useful for general measuring.

- Square—metal or wood ruler shaped like a "T" or an "L" and used for measuring right-angle corners; nice to have for cutting fabric panels.

- Steel tape—long, retractable, flexible ruler which can also be used as a rigid ruler when locked into position.

- Tape measure—flexible cloth or plastic tape.

- Yardstick (meterstick)—rigid ruler; also useful as a tool to smooth wrinkles out of fabric

when cutting large panels, and as a straight edge when marking cutting lines on fabric.

MARKING

These three kinds of markers come in handy:

- Chalk—for temporary marks on fabrics. Tailor's chalk is available in a small plastic holder, and as a dressmaker's marking pencil which can be sharpened to a point.

- Erasable marker—felt-tip marking pen which has evaporating or water-soluble ink.

- Pencil—an ordinary pencil makes a good marker for washable fabrics; marks show clearly and precisely until you wash them out.

WORK SPACE

When working with large amounts of fabric, it may be

necessary to expand your usual work space:

- Cutting board—sturdy laminated Kraft board which unfolds to 40" × 72" (101.5cm × 183cm). This board converts any flat surface to a large working area, and is marked with a grid for easy measuring and cutting.

- Padded worktable—if desired, make your own work surface for easier handling of large panels of fabric. Begin with a door or sheet of plywood supported by chairs or sawhorses, or use a picnic table. Pad the surface with cork, blankets, or batting. Cover the padding with muslin or a bed sheet, stapled to the underside of the surface to provide a smooth, taut working area. Use it for pressing as well as measuring, marking, and cutting.

CUTTING

To cut large expanses of fabric, have these cutting tools on hand:

- Dressmaker's shears—bent-handle shears let the fabric lie flat for accurate cutting; shears with long blades save cutting time.

- Pinking shears—useful for trimming the raw edges of ravel-prone fabrics.

- Razor—for cutting nonfabric materials such as cardboard. A single-edge razor blade or a hobby knife with a straight blade such as an X-acto® knife can be used.

- Rotary cutter and mat—the cutter has a circular blade attached to a handle, like a pizza cutter, and makes quick work of cutting straight fabric panels and bias or ruffle strips. A plastic mat which protects the cutting blade as well as the work surface is a necessity. Mats are available in sizes from 12″ × 18″ to 48″ × 96″ (30.5 × 46cm to 122 × 244cm) and roll up for compact storage.

- Small scissors—for trimming and clipping seams.

SEWING

Extras for Your Sewing Machine There are a number of machine attachments and accessories which can save you work and time, so they're worth buying if you don't already have them:

- Gathering foot—draws up the fabric to lock fullness into each stitch; a plus when gathering long ruffles or lace trims evenly.

- Hemming foot—scrolls the fabric to stitch a narrow hem automatically.

- Quilting foot—the short, open toes help you to follow marked lines when quilting fabric, and the adjustable spacing bar helps you sew evenly spaced lines of stitching. For some machines, the spacing bar is separate from the quilting foot.

- Ruffler attachment—makes quick work of gathering ruffles. There are many possible settings for different degrees of fullness. Some rufflers can be used to gather and apply ruffles in one step, and to make tiny pleats instead of gathers.

- Zipper foot—allows you to stitch very close to a raised edge. This foot is helpful not only for applying zippers, but also for stitching seams with welted insertions and applying other special tapes and trims.

Needles and Threads Choose your needle and thread according to the fabric you're sewing. Delicate fabrics need fine needles and threads, while heavier fabrics need coarser sizes. Also think about the number of fabric layers you'll be sewing. Home decorating projects may have four to six layers of fabric to sew at one time, making it sensible to use a larger-size needle and a coarser thread than normally indicated by the fabric type alone.

The chart below will help you select appropriate needles and threads for your sewing machine, and advise you about stitch length settings as well. When selecting machine needles, always use a *regular point* for woven fabrics. A *wedgepoint needle* works well on vinyls and synthetic suedes.

There are several kinds of threads on the chart for each fabric type. *Cotton-covered polyester thread* is a good, all-purpose choice, as is *100% polyester thread*. *Mercerized cotton* is most suitable for fabrics made from cotton, linen, silk, and wool fibers. However, it is not widely available.

In addition, you'll find *button and carpet thread* useful for making gathers and for sewing projects which need a heavy-duty thread. *Perle cotton yarn* is often used for handwork such as tying quilts and comforters; for this you'll need a special *large-eyed embroidery needle*. To install snap tape on a box spring for a dust ruffle, you'll need a *curved needle* for hand sewing.

Guide for Selecting Needles and Threads

FABRIC WEIGHT AND TYPE	THREADS	MACHINE NEEDLE SIZE (METRIC SIZE)	STITCHES PER INCH (CM)
Very Light: fine lace, ninon, organdy, voile	Extra-fine cotton-covered polyester; 100% polyester; mercerized cotton, size 50 or 60	9, 11 (70, 80)	15–20 (7–8)
Light: batiste, dotted Swiss, eyelet, handkerchief linen, lace, lightweight sheers	Extra-fine cotton-covered polyester; 100% polyester; mercerized cotton, size 50 or 60	11 (80)	12–15 (5–7)
Medium Light: gingham, satin, sheeting, soft synthetic suede	Cotton-covered polyester; 100% polyester; mercerized cotton, size 50 or 60	11 (80)	12–14 (5–6)
Medium: antique satin, baby and medium wale corduroy, broadcloth, chenille, chintz, damask, flannel, lace, moiré, muslin, piqué, sateen, taffeta, velvet, velveteen	Cotton-covered polyester; 100% polyester; mercerized cotton, size 50	11, 14 (80, 90)	12 (5)

Medium Heavy: fleece, quilted fabrics, textured linen weaves, synthetic suede	Cotton-covered polyester; 100% polyester; mercerized cotton, size 40 or 50	14, 16 (90, 100)	10–12 (4–5)
Heavy: duck, wide-wale corduroy, sailcloth	Extra-strong cotton-covered polyester; heavy-duty 100% polyester; mercerized cotton, size 40	16, 18 (100, 110)	8–10 (3–4)
Very Heavy: canvas, upholstery fabrics	Extra-strong cotton-covered polyester; heavy-duty 100% polyester; mercerized cotton size 8, 20, 30, or 40	18 (110)	8–10 (3–4)
Lightweight Vinyl	Cotton-covered polyester; 100% polyester	11, 14 (80, 90)	6–8 (3)
Heavyweight Vinyl	Extra-strong cotton-covered polyester; heavy-duty 100% polyester	14, 16 (90, 100) Also wedge-point	6–8 (3)

PRESSING

The basic equipment is an iron in good working order, and an ironing board. It's helpful to set up your ironing board with the wide end to your left. This gives you a larger pressing surface and leaves the tapered end of the board free for the iron.

In addition, you may need press cloths for adding moisture when fusing. You can cut your own from finely woven cheesecloth, or use a man's handkerchief. If you want to protect your fabric when pressing on the right side, cut a press cloth from muslin or purchase disposable press cloths.

Optional, but a true timesaver, is a metal bias tape pressing aid. Draw fabric strips through this funnel-shaped tool as you press to turn under the raw edges on custom-made bias tapes and bindings.

Sewing Supplies and Notions

The items described here are the kinds of special materials you'll need for many of the projects in this book, as well as for original projects born from your own creative thinking. Specific supplies and notions used for making the various kinds of window treatments are given in that section.

FILLERS

These are the different types of soft fillers often used for home decorating projects:

- Batting—used when quilting fabric or to fill quilts and comforters. There are two kinds of battings which are highly recommended for home decorating projects: *Needle-punched polyester batting* is dense and uniform, and similar to a blanket. A thin needle-punched batting is ideal for machine quilting, and a very puffy, high-loft type is perfect for tied quilts or comforters. *Bonded or glazed polyester batting* has a coating which makes it very stable and strong and, as with needle-punched battings, you can choose thin or high-loft versions. Battings can be purchased from a continuous roll by the yard (meter), precut in standard crib- and bed-size batts, and precut in small "craft" pieces which are sized right for small projects such as pillows or placemats.

- Polyester fiberfill—loose filler for making your own soft, plump pillow forms. Fiberfill won't lump or shift, is easy to work with, and is hand washable. It's sold in prepackaged amounts and priced by weight.

  Also available are ready-made polyester fiberfill pillow forms which are covered with muslin or bonded batting. You'll find these in many toss pillow sizes, from small 8½" (21.5cm) to large 30" (76cm) squares, and in round, rectangular, and heart shapes, too. There are rectangular pillows sized for standard (twin or double), queen, and king-size beds; small, round bed bolsters called neck rolls; and a 24" (61cm) square European bed pillow.

Polyurethane foam—solid filler for firm pillow forms which retain their shape. Ready-made foam forms can be purchased for toss pillows, wedge-shaped bolsters, and thick cushions used for seating. You can have foam cut to size where upholstery supplies are sold and make your own forms. Select the dense, extra-firm type of foam if making forms for seat cushions or modular pillow furniture. Foam forms should be covered with muslin or sheeting so the outer, decorative pillow cover fits smoothly. Some ready-made forms have this feature, but you can do it yourself easily, too. Shredded foam is also available for use as a loose filler when making your own pillow forms, but these pieces can be messy to handle, and will show through as lumps unless you use a firm, heavy fabric to cover your form.

TAPES

Some of these special tapes are used as closures, while others are timesaving construction aids:

- Hook and loop tape—self-gripping tape such as the Velcro® brand. You can purchase it by the yard (meter) from reels or in precut shorter lengths, and there are several colors including black and white. The self-adhesive version of this tape makes it easy to install fabric projects on hard surfaces such as sinks or vanity tables—stick the hook half of the tape to the hard surface, and stitch the loop half of the tape to the fabric project. The sew-on version of this tape makes a conve-

nient closure for pillow covers.

- Shirring tape—a convenient way to gather fabric. Stitch the tape to the project, then pull the strong cords woven into the tape to form gathers. The 2-cord shirring tape with a durable woven base is used for projects such as dust ruffles and headings on Austrian or balloon shades. The 4-cord shirring tape on a lightweight, mesh base is also used on Austrian and balloon shades for a wider gathered heading.

- Snap tape—has gripper snaps spaced at even intervals on a durable tape base. This tape can be used for closures on pillow covers, as well as for installing dust ruffles on box springs.

- Twill tape—strong tape used to reinforce seams. It comes in widths from ¼″ to 1″ (6mm to 2.5cm), in both black and white.

Quick Basting

A dressmaker's glue stick is a real timesaver when sewing for your home. Use the glue stick to hold tapes and trims in place for stitching and eliminate tedious hand basting.

Sewing Techniques

With a sewing machine and your sewing skills, you can create the many exciting projects in this book. All of the techniques are here—from making bias strips (along with a handy and unique chart for estimating bias yield) to cutting and sewing unusual fabrics, from appliqués to making welting. For the experienced home sewer, most of these techniques are old friends; for the beginner, they teach and sharpen skills during the creation of any project.

Appliqué by Machine

Using fusible web and zigzag stitching, fabric cutouts can be applied quickly and durably to decorate a background fabric. Dip into your assortment of scraps and remnants to appliqué texture-rich collages, unique toss pillows, or a quilt full of charm for the nursery. It's easy to design your own appliqués by cutting around fabric motifs or tracing illustrations from books. For the best results, keep appliqué outlines simple and choose fabrics that do not ravel easily.

PREPARING THE APPLIQUÉ

Cutting Appliqués sewn by machine require no seam allowances, so be sure to cut all appliqué shapes to their exact finished size. To do this, trace the outline of the appliqué on the right side of the appliqué fabric. Place a piece of fusible web on the wrong side of the appliqué fabric, and cut out both the appliqué and the web at the same time.

For fast and easy appliqués, make your fabric "fusible" by using a Norlon® pressing sheet to apply the web to your appliqué fabric before cutting out the appliqué.

Fusing Fuse the appliqué to the right side of the background fabric. Follow the manufacturer's instructions for the amount of heat, moisture, and pressure needed for a sound bond.

STITCHING THE APPLIQUÉ

General Directions Use a narrow, closely spaced zigzag stitch (satin stitch) to form a smooth, solid edge around the appliqué. Study the machine manual to adjust your sewing machine for the proper stitch length, width, and spacing. There may be a special presser foot with your machine for satin stitching; use it if you have it. Match the thread to the appliqué, or use a thread color which contrasts both with the appliqué and background fabric to emphasize the outline.

For a professional finish, position the stitches so the needle just pierces the background fabric on the right-hand swing, completely covering the raw edge of the appliqué (A). Work slowly so you can control the path of the stitches.

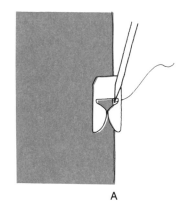

A

Corners For a smooth, solid finish at outside corners, stitch until the needle swings to the right, just at the corner (B). With the needle in the background fabric, raise the presser foot, pivot the fabric, and lower the presser foot to continue stitching.

On inside corners, stitch past the corner only the distance of the width of the zigzag stitch (C). Stop stitching with the needle in the left position. Raise the presser foot, pivot the fabric, then lower the presser foot to continue stitching.

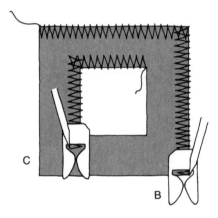

Points Gradually reduce the width of the stitches as you near a point (D), then increase the width as you stitch away from it with the following steps.

Stitch toward the point until the left swing of the needle falls on the background fabric instead of the appliqué. Reposition the fabric so the point is centered under the presser foot.

Decrease the stitch width so the stitching falls just on each side of the point. Continue de-creasing the stitch width to form the point.

Pivot the fabric, and continue stitching as you increase the stitch width until you return to the original width.

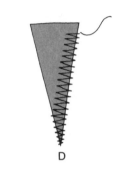

Curves Pivot the fabric slightly at frequent intervals to form a smoothly rounded edge.

For outside curves, pivot when the needle is on the right hand side of its swing, piercing the background fabric (E).

For inside curves, pivot when the needle is on the left hand side of its swing, piercing the appliqué (F).

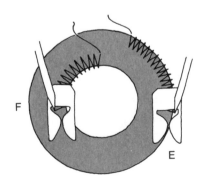

Bias Tapes and Bindings

Tap a fabric's hidden potential by cutting strips on the true bias grain. You'll create an adaptable and useful home decorating material—a binding pliant enough to encase straight or shaped edges smoothly, a custom covering for cording (see WELTING), and a practical facing for hems and curved edges. You can also use bias strips as band trims. If you're working with striped or plaid fabrics, the bias cut will form interesting diagonal lines with the fabric design.

The various techniques for making bias tapes and bindings are given below, but you can also purchase them precut in single-fold and double-fold versions, in various widths, and in a good selection of solid colors and prints. Single-fold bias tape is used for casings, band trims, and facings. Use double-fold bias binding to encase raw edges. The methods for applying purchased and custom-made tapes and bindings are the same.

PREPARING BIAS STRIPS

Cutting If you can make economical use of your fabric by cutting one bias strip for an entire project, this is ideal. However, most of the time it's necessary to piece strips. The chart on page 35 will help you estimate the bias yield from 1 yd (0.95cm) of fabric.

To cut bias strips, begin with a rectangle of fabric. Straighten the grain on the crosswise edges (see CUTTING FABRIC), and fold one crosswise edge so it is parallel to the selvage (A). The diagonal fold is on the fabric's true bias grain.

true bias · selvage · selvage · selvage · crosswise grain · lengthwise grain

A

Mark the fabric with cutting lines parallel to this fold (B). Determine the width of the strips as described below for single-fold bias tape and double-fold bias binding, or by the diameter of the cording for welting (see WELTING). Mark the short ends of each strip with a cutting line on the straight grain (C). Cut out the bias strips.

To piece the strips, place right sides together and stitch a ¼" (6mm) seam (D). This seam should be on the straight fabric grain, and small triangles will extend past each end of the seam. Press the seam open, and trim the triangles even with the strip (E).

For a large quantity of bias, such as when trimming curtain ruffles or binding the edge of a bedspread, instead of piecing all the bias strips separately you can make a continuous bias strip.

Begin with a rectangle of fabric which is at least twice as long as it is wide to make the most efficient use of this technique. Mark off the cutting lines as if you were making individual bias strips. Cut off triangles at each end of the rectangle (F), and use these to cut separate bias strips if desired.

In addition, mark a ¼" (6mm) seamline at each straight grain edge. Pin the straight grain edges with right sides together, staggering them so one strip's width extends beyond the seam at each end. The fabric will form a slightly twisted tube. Stitch the ¼" (6mm) seam, then press the seam open (G). Begin cutting at one end, and continue around the tube (H).

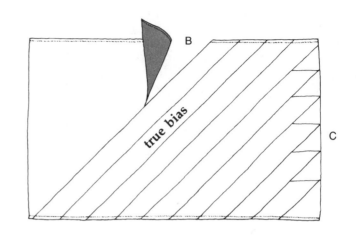

B

true bias

C

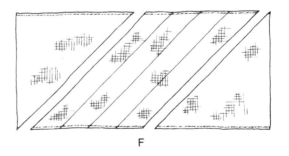

D

E

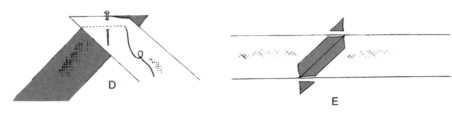

F

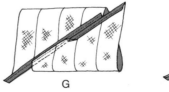

G

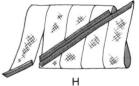

H

Removing the Slack Fabric cut on the bias grain stretches, so take out the extra slack by gently stretching the bias strips as you press them. This makes the strips slightly narrower, but eliminates wobbling seamlines and puckered bindings, so it's an important pre-application step. Since your fabric stretches a great deal on the bias grain, cut the strips about ¼ to ⅜" (6 to 10mm) wider to allow for removing the slack. If you've purchased bias binding, the slack has already been removed.

Preshaping Preshape bias tapes and bindings to make it easier to apply them to curved edges. Lay the bias tape or binding on top of the project edge, and steam press as you stretch and mold it into a matching shape.

APPLYING

Single-fold Bias Tape Use this method to make bias strips for casings, hem facings, or band trims.

Cut the bias strips the desired finished width, plus ½" (13mm) for turning under the raw edges and plus ¼" to ⅜" (6 to 10mm) for removing the slack. Turn the long raw edges under ¼" (6mm) and press. You can do this quickly with a bias tape pressing aid (I).

To use as a hem facing, trim the project hem allowance to ¼" (6mm). Right sides together, line up the raw edges of the bias tape and the project, and stitch a ¼" (6mm) seam (J). Press the bias tape to the wrong side. Edgestitch the remaining bias fold in place by machine (K).

Where the ends of the tape meet, lap them like band trims (see TRIMS). To use the tape as a band trim, or to miter corners, use the methods for band trims.

To use the tape as a casing, use the applied casing method (see CASINGS).

Double-fold Bias Binding Use this machine-applied method to bind raw edges. It makes a practical as well as decorative border, and is reversible.

Cut the bias strips twice the desired finished width, plus ½" (13mm) for turning under the raw edges and plus ¼" to ⅜" (6 to 10mm) for removing the slack. Turn the long raw edges under ¼" (6mm); press. Fold the binding lengthwise so the bottom extends slightly beyond the top (L). Press.

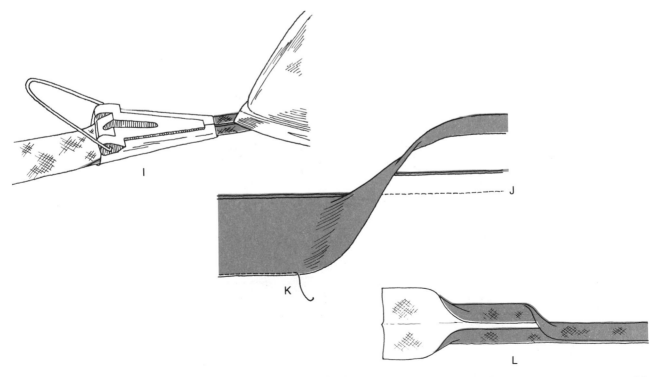

Trim the seam or hem allowance from the project edge. Slip the binding in place so it encloses the project raw edge, with the extended edge of the binding on the underneath or wrong side of the project. Stitch close to the edge from the right side, through all layers, to apply the binding with a single row of machine stitches (M).

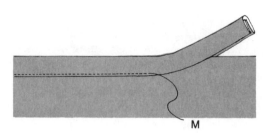

For outside corners, use a double miter. Stitch the binding to the edge of the corner (N). Fold the binding diagonally on both sides to form the miter (O). Resume stitching close to the edge. If desired, slipstitch the mitered fold by hand.

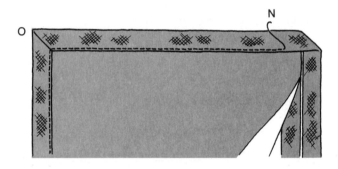

To join the binding ends which meet, use a lapped seam (P). So you won't have to rip out stitches for this, leave a short amount of the binding unstitched at the beginning and the end of your application. Trim the overlap on the straight grain, allowing enough fabric to turn under the raw edge ¼" (6mm). Also trim the underlap on the straight grain.

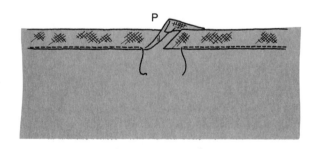

To complete bindings at a finished edge, trim the binding ends and fold under the edges of the binding about ¼" (6mm) (Q). Trim the project edges diagonally to remove bulk, and stitch close to the edge of the binding (R).

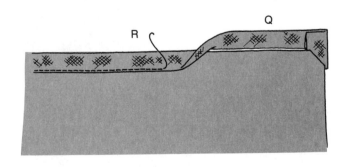

Estimating Bias Yield

This chart will help you to estimate how many individual bias strips can be cut from 1 yd (0.95m) of fabric. Five handy cutting widths for bias strips are given. The cutting widths include ½" (13mm) for turning under each raw edge ¼" (6mm), and an additional ¼" (6mm) for removing the slack:

- Strips cut 1¼" (3.2cm) wide can be used for ¼" (6mm) double-fold bias binding or ½" (13mm) single-fold bias tape.

- Strips cut 1¾" (4.5cm) wide can be used for ½" (13mm) double-fold bias binding or 1" (2.5cm) single-fold bias tape.

- Strips cut 2¼" (5.7cm) wide will cover ¼" (6mm) cable cord for welting or make ¾" (20mm) double-fold bias binding.

- Strips cut 2¾" (7cm) wide can be used for 1" (2.5cm) double-fold bias binding or 2" (5cm) single-fold bias tape.

- Strips cut 3¾" (9.5cm) wide can be used to cover ¾" (20mm) cord for welting.

1 YD (0.95M) OF FABRIC THIS WIDTH:	YIELDS THIS AMOUNT OF BIAS STRIPS (PIECED SEPARATELY)*				
	Cut 1¼"** (3.2cm) wide	Cut 1¾"** (4.5cm) wide	Cut 2¼"** (5.7cm) wide	Cut 2¾"** (7cm) wide	Cut 3¾"** (9.5cm) wide
35" (90cm)	23 yds (21.10m)	15 yds (13.80m)	12 yds (11m)	10 yds (9.15m)	8 yds (7.35m)
45" (115cm)	30 yds (27.50m)	21½ yds (19.70m)	16 yds (14.70m)	14 yds (12.90m)	10 yds (9.15m)
54" (140cm)	37 yds (33.90m)	26 yds (23.80m)	20 yds (18.30m)	16½ yds (15.10m)	12 yds (11m)
60" (152cm)	40 yds (36.60m)	29 yds (26.60m)	22½ yds (20.60m)	19 yds (17.40m)	14 yds (12.90m)

*All yardages are approximate
**Including ¼" for slack

Casings

Casings are tunnels of fabric through which something—a dowel, a curtain rod, elastic, a drawstring—is placed so the fabric can be gathered to fit. It takes little more than parallel rows of machine stitches to make casings, which is one reason why they're a popular heading for rod-pocket curtains and valances.

MEASURING

The size of the casing is determined by the item which will be inserted. A quick way to decide how deep to make the casing is to wrap your fabric or a tape measure around the curtain rod, dowel, or other item to be inserted. To this measurement add enough extra to permit your fabric to slide easily over the item (especially if your fabric is heavy or bulky), plus ¼" to ½" (6 to 13mm) for turning under the raw edge. Be sure to include this casing allowance when measuring for curtains and valances.

SEAMS

When projects have seams which extend into the casing area, it's a good idea to trim the seam allowances to half their width inside the casing, particularly if your fabric is medium- or heavyweight. This reduces the bulk of the multiple fabric layers considerably.

Another good idea is anchoring the seam allowances in the casing area to make inserting a curtain rod or other item much easier. Use strips of fusible web to keep all the seam allowances open (A).

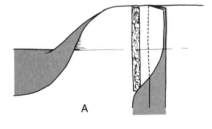

PLAIN

To make a plain casing, simply turn the raw edge under ¼" (6mm), then fold the fabric back on itself, wrong sides together. Stitch close to the bottom (B).

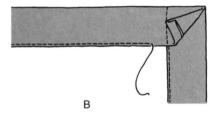

WITH SELF-RUFFLE

Allow extra casing fabric for a self-ruffle—twice the depth of the ruffle heading, in addition to the depth of the casing, plus ¼" to ½" (6 to 13mm) to turn under the raw edge. Stitch close to the long edge, and then stitch parallel to the edge to form the casing (C).

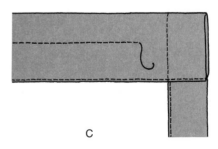

APPLIED

A separate strip of lightweight fabric can be stitched to the wrong side of a project to form a casing. Single-fold bias tape is often used for this (see BIAS TAPES AND BINDINGS).

To prepare the fabric strip, turn under the long edges ¼" (6mm) and press (if using purchased bias tape, this step has already been completed). Also turn under the short ends ½" (13mm) and press.

To apply the casing to a project edge, turn the raw edge of the project ½" (13mm) to the wrong side and press. Place the fabric strip on the project, wrong sides together, so the edges of both project and strip meet. Stitch close to both long edges of the fabric strip to make the casing. Leave the short ends open to insert the curtain rod, elastic, drawstring, or other item (D).

To apply the casing away from a project edge, place the fabric strip on the project, wrong sides together, in the desired position. Stitch close to both long edges of the fabric strip, leaving the short ends open as above.

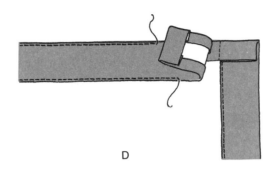

D

INSERTING A DRAWSTRING

Cording, rope, braid, self-fabric ties, ribbon—many different materials can be used for drawstrings. Make the casing deep enough to fit the drawstring easily, and before sewing the casing, make an opening for the drawstring. This could be two buttonholes, an opening in a seam, or large, hammer-on metal eyelets called grommets. The openings will stand up to wear longer if you add a small piece of fusible interfacing on the wrong side as a reinforcement before making them. Insert the drawstring through the opening with a safety pin.

INSERTING ELASTIC

To insert elastic into a casing, leave part of the casing edge unstitched to provide an opening (E), or leave an opening in a seam. For a crisp, well-defined edge, stitch close to the top edge of the casing.

Draw elastic through the opening with a safety pin, lap the elastic ends, and stitch securely (F). Stitch the opening closed (G).

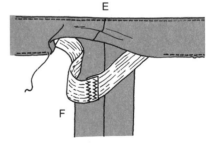

E

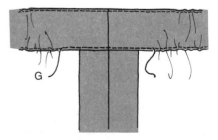

F

G

Cutting Fabric

Checking to see if your fabric shrinks and straightening the fabric grain are early steps in every home decorating project. They're vital—so don't skip them, even if you're anxious to get started.

PRESHRINKING

It's important to find out how much your fabric will shrink before you start cutting. Cut a large scrap—as large as 12" (30.5cm) square if you can spare it. Measure the scrap. Launder it if it's washable; steam press it if it's dry-cleanable. Measure again to determine shrinkage.

Even if your fabric is labeled preshrunk, it can shrink even further. The amount of residual shrinkage should be noted on the label. If it is 1 percent to 2 percent, this will have little effect on a pillow cover, but if you're making full-length curtains, this small amount of shrinkage could cause the curtains to become too short after laundering or dry cleaning.

If your scrap shows enough shrinkage to measure, preshrink the fabric or allow for shrinkage by making deeper hems in your project. The best way to preshrink home furnishing fabrics is by sending them to the dry-cleaner for steaming. This is more likely to preserve special stain repellent finishes and the fresh, new look of the fabric. If you're using a washable fashion fabric, and there are no special finishes to worry about, launder the fabric to preshrink it.

STRAIGHTENING THE GRAIN

A fabric which is off-grain must be straightened if the project is to hang correctly. This is especially true for window treatments. Before cutting, check to see if your fabric is on-grain by pulling a thread on each crosswise edge. Cut across the fabric on these threads for grain-perfect edges. Fold the fabric lengthwise, lining up the selvages on top of one another. If the grain is straight, the fabric lie flat without bubbles or ripples, and the crosswise edges will line up with each other. Pull the fabric gently on the bias to make it lie flat if necessary. Stubbornly off-grain fabrics can be more easily manipulated when slightly damp.

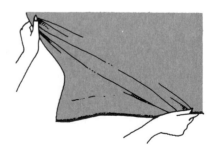

CUTTING LAYOUTS

Two types of fabrics need extra attention at the cutting stage—napped fabrics that have a one-way design, surface texture, or shading; and fabrics with designs which must be balanced visually and matched at seams.

Fabrics with Nap Strictly speaking, napped fabrics have a plush surface (corduroy and velvet), a brushed surface (fleece and synthetic suede), or a hairy surface (fur). For sewing purposes, however, the term is applied very broadly to all fabrics with a directional nature: designs which have a distinct one-way quality such as a scenic print; fabrics with shiny or lustrous surfaces which reflect light, such as polished cotton, satin, and damask; and fabrics such as brocade and slubbed linen which have a sculptured or textured surface.

For all fabrics in this category, cut out project sections so the nap—surface texture or design—heads in the same direction throughout the project. Mark the selvage with chalk arrows if you need reminders of the nap direction when cutting out large projects.

If the fabric has a soft surface, the direction in which it feels smoother is "with the nap." For the richest, deepest color shading, cut out project sections so the nap runs up, or feels smoother as you stroke it toward the top of the project.

Home decorating projects don't need extra fabric to follow a "with-nap" layout for cutting. Invariably, project sections are simple rectangles. These require the same amount of fabric whether or not they are cut in one direction only.

Please note! When folding napped fabrics crosswise for cutting, don't forget this additional step: for the nap to flow in the same direction on both fabric layers, cut along the crosswise fold and turn the upper layer around (A).

A

Fabrics with Large Design Repeats Prints, plaids, and stripes add an extra dimension to decorator fabrics, and they require a little extra thinking at the beginning of a project.

Because you'll have to position the motifs of a print and the bars of a plaid or stripe carefully for a pleasing visual balance, and line up adjoining fabric panels so the designs match at the seams, you'll need more fabric than if you were using a solid, plain fabric. To estimate how much extra, measure the length of the repeating unit of a plaid or print, or the crosswise measurement of a stripe's repeat. A good rule of thumb is to buy an extra amount equal to one repeat for each seam or panel in your project.

As you cut out project sections, use a with-nap layout as described earlier. With all the pieces headed in the same direction, you'll never have to worry whether a plaid is even or uneven, or whether print motifs are one way. Any fabric design will line up uniformly.

Center prominent motifs, the strongest stripe, or the most dominant bar of a plaid. Also try to avoid cutting off motifs at the top and bottom of a project. If this doesn't work out, position a complete motif where it's most prominent, and a partial motif where it's least noticeable. On a full-length window treatment, for example, place the complete motif at the heading and the cut-off motif at the hem (B). On a sill-length window treatment, place the complete motif at the hem and the partial motif at the heading (C).

At seams, match the fabric design on the *seamline*, not at the raw edge (D), so the design will line up properly as you sew.

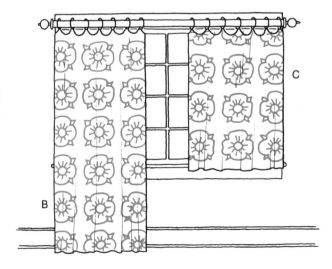

Fabrics That Require Special Handling

A number of home decorating fabrics need special handling or sewing techniques. Be assured there's no need to avoid these fabrics—many of the special methods are actually shortcuts. Another favorable point: some of the most attractive room settings result from a fabric choice that's out of the ordinary.

LACE

With a built-in beauty and elegance, lace can make a simple project very special. One traditional showcase for lace panels is at the window, with sew-on rings or a plain casing for a curtain heading; the lace motifs form a stunning display as they filter the sunlight. Lace can also be backed with colorful satin, taffeta, or fine batiste for pillows and bed covers, or laid over a separate undercloth for the table. Gathered lushly, lace makes romantic ruffles to trim curtains or a canopy, and provides the major ingredient for a deluxe vanity skirt or an heirloom bassinet ensemble.

Cutting Many laces have a net background, and can be cut either crosswise or lengthwise. Eyelet lace is a finely woven fabric with an embroidered lace-like open design; most eyelet laces have a border along one lengthwise edge.

Focus on the lace motifs to devise your layout. Center prominent motifs, match them at the seams for a unified flow, and place any finished decorative borders at project edges to eliminate the need for hems.

Stitching Use a #11 (80) machine needle, a fine thread, and a short stitch length of 12–15 stitches per inch (2.5cm) for delicate laces. For other laces, a #14 (90) needle, regular sewing thread and 10–12 stitches per inch (2.5cm) can be used.

Seams Make French seams or narrow interlocking seams to preserve the sheer quality of a lace. A twice-stitched seam makes a very sheer finish, and since the raw lace edges won't ravel, a practical choice as well.

Mock French seams can also be used (see SEAMS).

An appliqué seam—an alternative for net-background laces—makes a practically invisible joining. Lap the lace edges, matching the seamlines and motifs. Trim the uppermost layer along a motif (A). Use a narrow, closely spaced zigzag to stitch the trimmed edge in place (B), then trim the underlap close to the stitches.

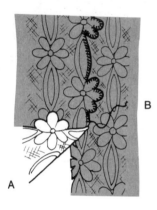

Hems A wide, double hem (see HEMS) can be used on an all-over lace, treating the fabric like any other sheer.

To use the lace border at the hemline, just trim any stray threads off the border motif. No further finish is needed.

Lace borders can also be cut out and appliquéd for the hem. Stitch with a close, narrow zigzag as described above for the appliqué seam.

SHEERS AND OPEN WEAVES

Light and airy sheers look their best when gathered to maximum fullness—for rod-pocket curtains, for a feminine dust ruffle, or for a tiered bedspread. Some of the most popular sheers for home decorating are organdy, dotted Swiss, voile, and batiste. Open-weave fabrics are often used for curtains. Be careful if using a fiberglass, open-weave fabric. The fabric is very perishable because of the open weave. Handle it carefully when sewing, and be especially careful when washing it.

Cutting If the selvage is neat and even, and did not pucker during preshrinking, you have the option of placing the selvage at a project edge and eliminating a hem or seam finish. For curtains, however, it's better to trim off the selvage. It is more tightly woven than the rest of the fabric and could distort the way the fabric hangs and drapes.

To prevent the fabric from slipping and sliding as you cut, delicate sheers and open weaves can be pinned to a cutting board, or the cutting surface can be covered with a sheet. Use fine silk pins to avoid damaging the fabric, and sharp shears—dull ones "chew" these fabrics.

Stitching Use a #11 (80) needle, fine thread, and a short stitch length of 12–15 stitches per inch (2.5cm). A needle plate with a small hole prevents the fabric from bunching as you begin to stitch and helps prevent seams from puckering. If seams on very lightweight sheers do pucker, or if the fabric is slippery, stitch with tissue paper between fabric and machine; tear away tissue after stitching.

Seams Seams should be narrow and finished to conceal the raw edges. French, mock French, and interlocking seams (see SEAMS) are recommended for sheers and open weaves.

Hems Hems can be very narrow or very wide (see HEMS). Make wide hems double to hide the raw edges.

SYNTHETIC SUEDE

The rich look of synthetic suede makes it a favorite for room accessories, trims such as bindings, luxurious window treatments, and bed and table coverings. It's a pleasure to sew, because the raw edges don't ravel. Lightweight, supple synthetic suedes such as Glore™-valcana, Lamous®, and Facile™ can be sewn with ordinary methods, although a with-nap layout is necessary for uniform color shading (see CUTTING LAYOUTS). For heavier types such as Ultrasuede®, you'll need a with-nap layout plus the modified sewing methods given here.

Cutting As you cut out project sections, run the nap up for the deepest color. Use sharp shears for clearly cut edges, and mark cutting lines with tailor's chalk.

Stitching Use a fine #11 (80) or a #14 (90) sewing machine needle and a medium stitch length of 10–12 stitches per inch (2.5cm). Hold the fabric taut in front and in back of the presser foot to feed the fabric evenly and prevent puckered seams.

Seams Conventional plain seams can be used on synthetic suedes. Use a narrow strip of fusible web to hold the seam allowances open and flat against the fabric (A). Or the seams may be topstitched open (B), or to one side (C), as desired.

Lapped seams, topstitched like those on real leather, have a more casual appearance. For this special seam, trim the seam allowance from one project section. Plan ahead so all the seams lap in the same direction. Mark the seam line on the adjoining section with chalk, and lap the trimmed seam allowance to this line. Place a narrow strip of fusible web between the two fabric layers and press lightly to steam baste them (D), or use a glue stick to hold the fabric layers in place. Topstitch close to the overlapping edge and ¼" to ½" (6 to 13mm) away (E).

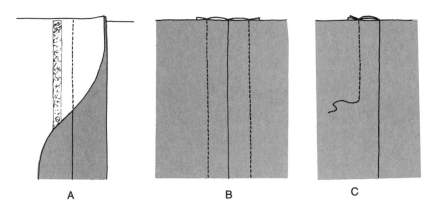

A   B   C

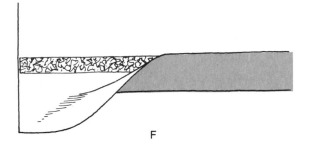

F

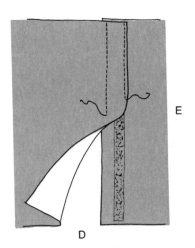

E

D

Hems For a plain hem, turn up 1" to 1½" (2.5 to 6.5cm) and fuse in place with a narrow strip of fusible web (F).

For a less bulky hem, trim off the hem allowance and topstitch the edge to prevent stretching (G).

For a faced hem that adds weight to the bottom, cut a self-fabric strip ½" (13mm) wide, shaped to match the hem edge. Topstitch to the hem edge, with wrong sides together (H).

Pressing Press on the wrong side of the fabric, with a synthetic temperature setting on your iron and lots of steam. Use a press cloth to protect the fabric. If it's necessary to press on the right side, use a self-fabric press cloth to preserve the luxurious nap.

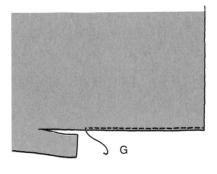

G

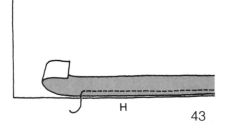

H

QUILTED FABRICS

Quilted fabrics provide warmth and have an interesting surface design. They're most often used for bed coverings and table accessories. The key to sewing quilted fabrics is dealing with their bulkiness, and the following cutting and sewing tips show you how.

Cutting Because of the thickness of quilted fabrics, it's easier and more accurate to cut out one layer of fabric at a time. Plan to match the quilting design at the seams, in addition to any prominent woven or printed fabric motifs, for the most professional look.

Stitching Use a slightly long stitch, about 8–10 stitches per inch (2.5cm), and a #14 (90) or #16 (100) needle, depending upon the thickness of your quilted fabric.

Seams After stitching a seam, trim the batting from the seam allowances. To do this, pick out the quilting stitches in the seam allowances and peel apart the layers to expose the batting. Finish the raw edges of the top and backing fabrics using the techniques for mock French or twice-stitched seams (see SEAMS).

Hems To eliminate bulky hems, quilted projects can be lined to the edge. Edges can also be encased in double-fold bias binding, or finished with a single-fold bias tape hem facing (see BIAS TAPES AND BINDINGS).

A self-finished hem is another alternative. For this special method, trim the hem allowance to ⅜" (10mm). Top-stitch 1" (2.5cm) from the edge, and pick out the quilting stitches beneath this topstitched line (A). Pull the thread ends to the inside and knot them together. Trim the batting close to the topstitching (B). Turn under the raw edges of the top and backing fabrics ⅜" (10mm) and edgestitch them together (C).

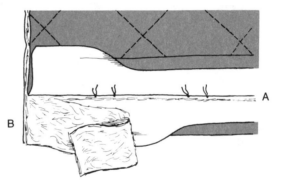

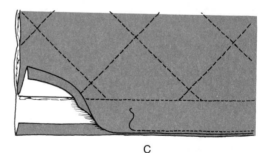

VINYL AND OTHER PLASTICS

Vinyl and other plastics might be smooth-surfaced, or textured to mimic other materials such as leather. Because they're waterproof and wipe clean, they make practical shower curtains, table coverings, and placemats. Two important points control how you handle these fabrics—pins and needles leave permanent holes, and plastics melt under the heat of an iron.

Cutting Cut out one layer of fabric at a time using sharp shears, a rotary cutter, or a single-edge razor blade. Instead of pins, use masking tape or weights to hold patterns or templates in place. Or draw your cutting lines directly onto the fabric with chalk. Don't use a tracing wheel for marking—it can leave a permanent mark.

Stitching Use a # 11 (80) or #14 (90) needle for lightweights, and a #14 (90) or #16 (100) for heavier weights. Wedgepoint needles help prevent splitting the fabric, although regular sharp-point needles can be used on plastics that have a fabric backing.

To keep needle perforations to a minimum, use a long stitch, about 6–8 stitches per inch (2.5cm). Tie thread ends to begin and complete a line of stitching—backstitching weakens these fabrics.

Instead of pin-basting, use masking tape, paper clips, or a glue stick to hold fabric layers in position for sewing (place the tape so you won't stitch through it and gum up the needle). If the fabric sticks as you feed it under the needle, sandwich it between two layers of tissue paper for stitching and tear off the tissue afterward.

Seams A lapped seam, as described earlier for synthetic suedes, works best on plastics. Omit the fusible web and "baste" with masking tape instead.

Hems Heavy plastics need no hems—just trim the edge evenly on the hemline. On others, a topstitched hem 1" to 2" (2.5 to 5cm) deep is suitable; just trim the hem allowance evenly, turn up the hem, and topstitch close to the cut edge. Edges can also be encased in double-fold bias binding (see BIAS TAPES AND BINDINGS).

Pressing Finger pressing is usually all that is needed. To use an iron to press, select a low heat setting without steam; cover the fabric with a press cloth to prevent damage.

Fusing Techniques

Thanks to their heat-sensitive chemistry, fusible interfacings and webs can save you time and stitches. Fusing also makes fabrics more crisp, and this is precisely the quality needed for many home decorating applications. Be sure your iron is in good health, because plenty of heat and steam makes the soundest bond.

Firm, opaque fabrics are the best candidates for fusing methods. Do not fuse sheers, laces, open-weave fabrics, vinyls, or plastics.

FUSIBLE INTERFACINGS

Fusible interfacings have a resin coating on one side which melts under heat, moisture, and pressure to fuse the interfacing to a fabric. A great many different types of fusible interfacings are available for sewing, from whisper-weight sheers to heavy craft weights, from soft and supple types to firm, crisp varieties.

To select a fusible interfacing, read the bolt labels and the plastic interleaving which manufacturers include with their products. You'll find suggested uses and suitable fabric types listed to help you make a good interfacing choice. Also, most fusibles are labeled either "soft" or "crisp," describing the two different degrees of stiffness. Picture your completed project, decide which effect you desire, and choose accordingly. However, to be sure you've made the correct interfacing choice,

it's important to test-fuse a sample before you sew.

Making a Sample Test the effect of a fusible interfacing on fabric scraps before cutting out project sections. During this trial run, as well as during the actual fusing later, follow the interfacing manufacturer's directions precisely, to the point of counting by the clock the number of seconds suggested. The most permanent bonds come from applying the heat, moisture, and pressure for the right length of time.

Applying Trim the interfacing ⅛" (3mm) from seamlines in the seam allowances, and trim off corners diagonally to reduce bulk. When using a heavy interfacing, trim off the entire seam allowance to reduce bulk.

Position the interfacing resin (shiny) side down down on the wrong side of the fabric. If fusing a large piece, steam baste the interfacing into position by pressing lightly with the tip of the iron in several places. To permanently fuse, press down firmly, following the manufacturer's directions. Lift up the iron and overlap the previous area to fuse large pieces. Let the fused piece cool completely before handling it.

FUSIBLE WEB

Available by the yard (meter) or in precut strips, fusible webs are versatile, useful bonding agents. Use them for fabric-to-fabric bonding, to apply ribbons and other straight trims, or to apply fabric to wood, metal, or cardboard for coordinated accessories. The item you are applying the web to must not be sensitive to heat.

Applying Simply layer the web between the materials to be fused, and steam press, following the web manufacturer's directions. The web should melt completely for a sound bond, and will not be visible between the two fused materials.

Fuse hems as described below; to use web for appliqués, see APPLIQUÉ BY MACHINE.

Hems For a plain hem, turn under the raw edge ¼" to ½" (6 to 13mm). Position a strip of web just below the top fold, (A), and fuse.

For a firm, crisp hem, fuse the entire hem allowance (B). Trim the web so it's slightly less than the depth of the hem, to avoid pressing on the top hem fold.

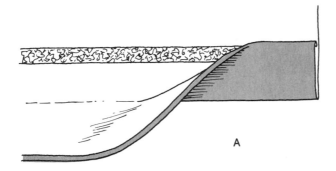

A

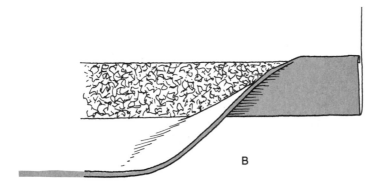

B

Troubleshooting

If your fusing isn't going as smoothly as you'd like, or the bond seems less than permanent, here are some helpful remedies:

- To add extra moisture, use a damp press cloth. A disposable press cloth, man's handkerchief, cotton muslin, or cheesecloth works well for this.

- To add heat, make a heat-reflective pressing surface by covering heavy cardboard with aluminum foil. This imitates the metal fusing plates used commercially.

- For thick fabrics, fuse following the manufacturer's instructions, then press again from the right side. Pressing the fabric on both sides helps the heat and moisture to penetrate more effectively.

- To remove fused interfacing if you've made a mistake, peel off the interfacing as you re-steam the area. Discard the interfacing, for it can't be used again. Two materials fused together with web can be peeled apart in a similar way.

- If web or fusing resins get on your iron, use the special cleaning products available in notion departments.

Gathers on a Large Scale

To handle gathers for large projects, these special tools and techniques should be part of your sewing repertoire. Whether you're fashioning a deep flounce for a bedspread, frills for the windows, or sweet confections for the nursery, you'll find the process goes much more smoothly, and takes far less time, if you adopt the methods given here.

WITH MACHINE AIDS

Gathering Foot With a gathering foot, the fabric is drawn up and the fullness locked into place with each straight stitch. The amount of gathering is controlled by adjusting the stitch length and the needle tension—increased tension and longer stitches create fuller gathers. Read the instructions in your sewing machine manual to learn which settings are possible on your machine.

Ruffler This machine attachment makes uniform gathers quickly and easily. Study the instructions that come with the ruffler to find out how to adjust the fullness—there are a great many possible settings. Usually there's a screw control to make the gathers more or less full as you stitch, in addition to adjustments in stitch length.

Explore the many capabilities of this attachment to learn other ways it can save you work, such as making a ruffle and applying it in one operation. Learn which setting makes small pleats, too, and use them as an alternative to gathers if you like the more tailored effect and if it suits your fabric.

WITH SHIRRING TAPE

This special-purpose tape has rows of strong cord threaded through it. Use shirring tape for headings on valances, Austrian shades, and dust ruffles.

It's simple to apply—pick out the cords at each end of the tape, and turn under the raw edges of the tape. Pin or baste the tape in position on the wrong side of your fabric. Stitch around the edges of the tape with a zipper foot (A). If you're applying 2-cord or 4-cord shirring tape, also stitch between the cords. Keep the cord ends free.

To gather the fabric, knot the cords at one end and use small overcast stitches to secure the raw ends of the cord to the tape (B). Pull the cords from the other end of the tape, sliding the fabric into even gathers; tie a knot. For easy laundering or dry cleaning, don't cut off the long cord ends. Tuck the cords out of sight on the wrong side of the project. Wind the cords into a figure eight and secure with a rubber band to hide the long ends. You can then untie the knot so the fabric can be handled flat to launder.

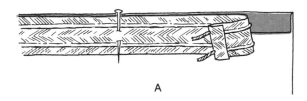

A

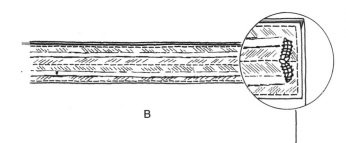

B

WITH ZIGZAG STITCHES

To gather with the confidence that the gathering thread won't break, use a wide zigzag stitch over narrow cord, string, or strong button-and-carpet thread on the wrong side of the fabric (A). Position the zigzag stitches so they fall completely within the seam allowance, just beyond the seamline, and be sure the stitches don't pierce the cord. After gathering the fabric, use a zipper foot to stitch the seam, then pull out the cord.

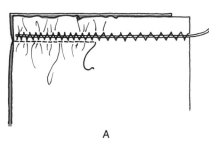

A

Easy Gathers with Straight Stitches

Modify the standard technique of using two rows of long machine stitches for gathering to make working on great lengths of fabric easier:

- If you divide the gathering stitches into workable segments, the gathering threads are less likely to break from the fabric weight and your handling. Pin-mark the edge to be gathered into equal parts—as many as eight or sixteen for long edges—and begin and end the gathering stitches at these points. For some projects, it may be more logical to stop the gathering stitches at seams. Avoid gathering fabric sections larger than about 2' to 3' (60 to 91.5cm) with a single length of thread. Secure one end of gathering threads by wrapping them around a straight pin in a figure eight or by tying them in a knot.

- Since the bobbin threads do the work when gathering, it's practical to fill the bobbin with a strong thread such as heavy-duty cotton/polyester thread. Buttonhole twist can also be used on some machines.

- If your fabric is fairly heavy, a third line of gathering stitches in the seam allowance can be a big help. The extra row of gathering stitches makes a good back-up in case either of the others breaks.

Hand Stitches

Although your sewing machine does the lion's share of stitching for home decorating projects, from time to time a touch of hand sewing is needed. If you've done some dressmaking, the techniques below probably are already among your skills.

OVERCASTING

This stitch is worked diagonally over raw edges or cord ends to prevent them from raveling. It can also be used to hold two edges together. Hold the needle at a slant to overcast an edge (A), spacing your stitches ⅛" to ¼" (3 to 6mm) apart.

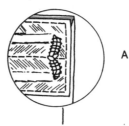

A

SLIPSTITCH

This stitch is often used to finish mitered corners on hems, bias bindings, and trims—places difficult to sew by machine. You can also use slipstitches to close seam openings.

To slipstitch, pick up a thread or two of fabric, then slide the needle through the folded edge before taking the next stitch (A). Take ⅛" to ¼" (3–6mm) long stitches for an invisible finish; use longer stitches on heavy or bulky fabrics.

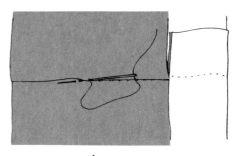

A

SWING TACK

Also called a French tack, this technique uses the chainstitch to make a thread chain which loosely holds together layers of fabric. Use a double thread or buttonhole twist.

Begin by fastening the thread to one fabric layer with a few small stitches (A). Take another stitch to make a loop (B). Reach through the first loop to pick up the thread, forming the second loop (C). Pull this second loop to tighten the chain. Continue pulling new loops through the old until the chain is of sufficient length for your project.

To finish, bring the needle through the last loop to make a knot (D). Fasten the thread to the second fabric layer with a few small stitches.

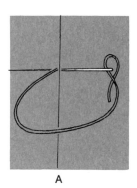

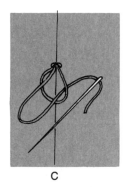
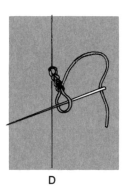

A   B   C   D

WHIPSTITCH

These tiny, slanted stitches are used to hold two edges together. Hold the needle at right angles to the edge to take the stitches, making the stitches very close together (A)—1/16" (2mm) or less apart.

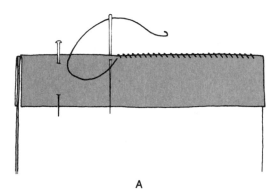

A

Hems

Putting in hems by machine is the fastest and most durable way to finish edges on home decorating projects. Blindstitching and topstitching are the most common methods used. If the hems are straight, they can also be fused (see FUSING TECHNIQUES).

Certain projects need hems which are special because they're very narrow or very wide. The most useful methods for making these hems are given below.

BLINDSTITCHING

The blindstitch is a stitch pattern built into many sewing machines. It usually combines straight stitches with periodic zigzag stitches, and makes an inconspicuous hem for a quality finish. Set your machine for 10–12 stitches per inch (2.5cm) and a narrow to medium stitch width.

Prepare a hem for blindstitching by pressing under the raw edge at the top of the hem at least ½" (13mm). Baste or pin the hem in place ¼" (6mm) from the top edge. Fold back the bulk of the fabric to expose the hem edge. As you sew, the straight stitches should fall on the hem edge, and the points of the zigzag stitches should pierce one or two threads of the project (A). If the stitches are too large on the right side of the project, decrease the stitch width.

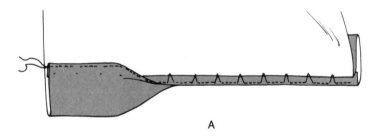

A

TOPSTITCHING

A straight stitch can be used for hems, although the stitching shows on the right side. For a topstitched hem, turn under the raw edge ¼" to ½" (6 to 13mm), press the hem in position for sewing, and topstitch along the folded-under raw edge.

NARROW HEMS

Use a narrow hem when you wish to avoid the weight a deep hem adds to a project (such as when making ruffles) and for curved edges where deeper hems are difficult to ease (such as on round tablecloths).

With a Hemmer Foot This special presser foot automatically scrolls the fabric as it feeds under the needle, folding the raw edge under twice (A). Trim the hem allowance to ¼" (6mm) so the finished hem will be ⅛"

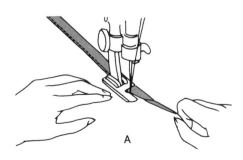

A

(3mm) wide. For an easy start, finger press the hem into stitching position for an inch (2.5cm) or two at the beginning.

Without a Hemmer Foot This method takes extra time, because the hem must be folded into position before stitching.

Trim the hem allowance to ⅝" (15mm). Turn up the hem ⅝" (15mm) and press, easing in fullness if necessary. Turn under the raw edge so that the edge lies along the first crease (B); press. Stitch along the upper fold (C).

With Decorative Machine Stitches Embroidery-type machine stitches can be used as alternatives to narrow hems. Select a dense type such as a zigzag satin stitch or scallop stitch. Stitch on the hemline, trimming away the excess hem allowance close to the stitching afterward.

For this treatment, it's a good idea to test the decorative stitch on scraps first. If the fabric draws up, back the fabric with tissue paper, then tear the tissue away after stitching.

WIDE HEMS

Many times a wide hem improves the way fabric drapes, since it adds extra weight along the hemmed edge. This is especially true for curtains—bottom hems 3" wide is a good rule of thumb. Side hems which are about 1" (2.5cm) wide help strengthen and support the fabric in these situations. The amount of fabric used in hems such as these can add up, so be sure to allow for them when estimating fabric requirements.

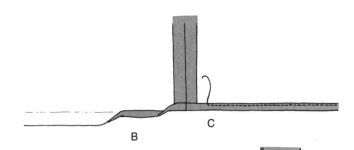

B

C

Plain Hem Turn under the raw edge ¼" to ½" (6 to 13mm), fold the hem, and blindstitch or topstitch the hem in place (D).

Double Hem Use this type of hem to add more weight, or to hide the raw edge on sheers. Begin by cutting a double-width hem allowance. Fold the raw edge under the depth of the hem, then fold the hem under again. Machine blindstitch or topstitch the hem in place, or slipstitch the hem by hand (E).

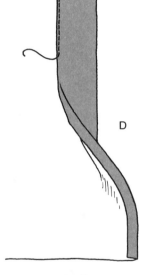

D

Adding Weights Drapery weights improve the way curtains hang, and are easy to add. In general, add weights to the hem at corners and seams. Sew-on weights can be loosely hand sewn to the back of the hem; clip the stitches and remove the weights to launder or dry-clean the project.

On sheer, full-length curtains, use a double hem and don't miter the corners. You can then slip a covered chain weight inside the hem fold. Use hand stitches to tack the chain lightly at corners and seams.

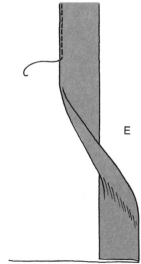

E

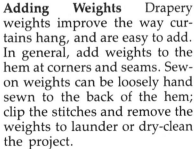

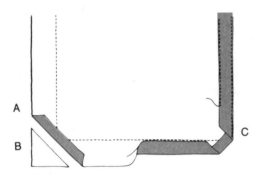

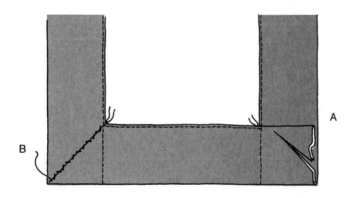

MITERING CORNERS ON HEMS

Narrow Hems After turning up and pressing the hem allowances, fold the fabric diagonally across the corner (A). Trim a triangle from the point, leaving ¼" (6mm) (B). As the narrow hem is folded under on each edge, the corner will miter (C).

Wide Hems Hem both sides all the way to the edge. Hem the crossing sides, starting and stopping the machine stitching at the first hemmed edges (A). Pull threads to the wrong side and knot. Fold the corner under to form the miter. Trim off the excess fabric to leave ¼" to ½" (6 to 13mm) turned under at the miter. Slipstitch the miter fold by hand (see HAND STITCHES) (B).

Quilting by Machine

Quilting—stitching together two fabrics with batting or another soft filler sandwiched in between—is one way to create a warm bed covering or an energy-conserving window treatment. The quilted layers trap air very effectively, even when lightweight fabrics are used. Quilting also adds a rich surface texture to otherwise plain fabrics, making it a favorite technique for items such as valances, pillows, and placemats, and adds body to sheets and similar fabrics which otherwise would be too lightweight or soft for a project.

For machine quilting, use a nonbulky filler such as a thin batting, flannel, fleece, or a lightweight blanket. Finish the quilting first, before cutting out project sections or panels. Small pieces are easier to quilt. Also, since quilting "puffs up" a fabric and reduces the dimensions, cutting after you quilt is more precise.

PREPARING THE FABRIC LAYERS

Marking Use chalk, or pencil on washable fabrics, to mark the right side of the top fabric layer with diagonal lines from corner to corner crossing in the center, and with lines from the midpoints of each edge on the straight grain (A). These markings play a dual role: they're a basting guide, plus you'll follow them to make the first rows of quilting stitches. If you use a quilting foot or an adjustable space bar on your machine, as described below, no further markings are needed. If quilting without the foot or bar, mark all the lines for quilting at this point.

Basting Layer the fabrics as follows: backing fabric, right side

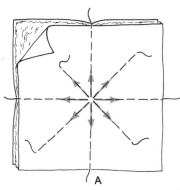

A

55

Quilting Large Areas

These tips make quilting large pieces of fabric easier:

- Work on the floor to stack the fabrics and filler for basting. Use a yardstick (meterstick) to smooth wrinkles from areas where your arms won't reach.

- Roll up the layers to the halfway point and baste the unrolled half from the center out. Roll up the basted half and unfurl the other side to finish basting.

- Add a support, such as a card table, behind your machine to hold the layers so they won't pull the portion under the presser foot out of line.

- To fit the bulk under your machine, you may find it necessary to tightly roll the portion on your right.

down; batting or other filler; top fabric, right side up. Make sure each layer is smooth and free of wrinkles.

By hand, baste the layers together with long, loose stitches following the basting lines marked on the top fabric. Work from the center to the edges to avoid creating a lump of filler or a fabric bubble in the middle. If your fabrics are slippery or the piece is large, add more rows of basting from the center to the edges to prevent the layers from shifting as you quilt.

MACHINE QUILTING

Setting Up the Machine Attach an adjustable spacing bar to your machine. If you have a quilting foot, the bar is part of the foot; the foot's short toes make quilting easier. A spacing bar can also be a separate accessory which attaches to the needle shaft.

To begin, test the stitch length, tension, and presser foot adjustment on a sample fabric/filler/fabric sandwich. For smooth quilting, you may have to use a longer stitch and decrease the pressure on the presser foot.

Diagonal Quilting To quilt a diamond pattern, follow the two corner-to-corner basted lines to stitch an "X." Use the spacing bar as a guide to stitch parallel rows on both sides of the first two lines (B).

Square Quilting To quilt a pattern of squares, follow the two center lines basted on the straight grain to stitch a "+." Use the spacing bar as a guide to stitch parallel rows on both sides of these first two lines (C).

Channel Quilting To quilt a pattern of parallel rows, follow one of the center lines basted on the straight grain for the first line of stitching. Use the spacing bar as a guide to stitch parallel rows on both sides (D). To keep the fabric from puckering between the stitching lines, begin stitching each row at the completed edge of the previous row.

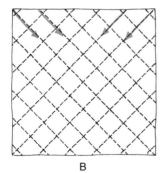

B

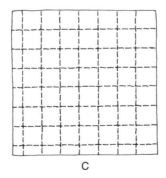

C

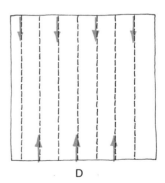

D

Ruffles

Ruffles add a romantic, feminine flourish to many projects. On the practical side, ruffles can add length to a window treatment or table covering, and increase the size of a pillow. They're economical trims because you make them yourself from matching or contrasting fabric.

Soft, lightweight fabrics in solid colors or small prints make the best ruffles. Crisp fabrics may not fall in graceful folds when ruffled, heavy fabrics may be too bulky once gathered, and large print designs will be lost unless the ruffle is very wide. Fabric border trims or lace edgings can also be used for ruffles, a convenience because they're precut into appropriate widths and need no piecing to achieve the necessary length. If you are making ruffles for curtains or other large projects, use the special gathering techniques to save time (see GATHERS ON A LARGE SCALE).

CUTTING

In general, cut fabric strips for ruffles on the straight, crosswise grain. The strips can be any width, from narrow to very wide. Remember to allow extra width for any seam allowances, hems, self-facings, or headings planned.

To estimate how long a fabric strip you'll need, measure the seam or edge to which the ruffle will be applied. Cut a strip twice as long for minimum fullness, and three times as long for a very full ruffle, piecing where necessary. Narrow ruffles look best with minimum fullness, but wide ruffles and those cut from sheer or lightweight fabrics look best when very full.

When estimating fabric for a project, you'll have to add an allowance for cutting ruffles. Use the formulas below to figure how much extra fabric is needed for ruffles cut crosswise.

On sheer fabrics, hems and all or most piecing can be eliminated by cutting the ruffle strips lengthwise. Use the selvage as the ruffle's finished edge. This is a wonderful timesaver, but be sure the selvage is neat and even, and did not pucker during preshrinking.

In a similar way, hems can be omitted on eyelet lace and lace edging trims if you use the prefinished lace border as the bottom edge of the ruffle.

PLAIN RUFFLES

Plain ruffles have one long edge which is finished, usually by a hem. The other long edge is gathered, then inserted in a seam or stitched to a project edge. When cutting fabric strips for a plain ruffle, add ⅝" (15mm) seam allowance and ⅝" (15mm) hem allowance to the width.

If it's necessary to piece the strips, use French seams (see SEAMS). If the two short edges are to be joined—such as when inserting a ruffle in the seams around a pillow—join them in a French seam to make a continuous ruffle. If the two short edges are not joined—such as

for a dust ruffle—narrow-hem them (see HEMS).

Use a narrow hem to finish one long edge of the ruffle (A). Or encase this edge in double-fold bias binding (see BIAS TAPES AND BINDINGS).

Prepare the other long edge for gathering with two rows of long machine stitches—one on the seamline, and one ¼" (6mm) away in the seam allowance (B).

Use pins to divide the project and the ruffle into equal parts—halves or quarters for small projects, eighths or more for larger ones. Matching the pin markers, pin the ruffle to the

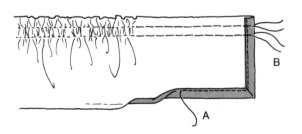

project with right sides together (C). Pull the bobbin threads to gather the ruffle evenly, and pin-baste. At any corners, ease in extra fullness so the ruffle won't cup at its outer edge once finished (D).

Inserting in a Seam Machine-baste the ruffle in place, positioning the stitches just inside the seamline in the seam allowance (E).

Pin the other project section on top so the right sides of the project sections are together and the ruffle is sandwiched in between (F). Stitch the seam. Remove the basting and gathering stitches, and grade the seam allowances (see SEAMS).

Applying to an Edge Following the instructions above, stitch the ruffle to the edge on the seamline, then press only the seam allowances to flatten the gathered fabric.

For a quick finish after applying the ruffle, trim the seam allowances to ¼" (6mm). Use a zigzag stitch to overcast the raw edges together (A). Press the ruffle away from the project.

For a more durable finish on straight edges, trim the ruffle seam allowance to ¼" (6mm). Fold under the project's seam allowance ¼" (6mm) and bring the fold to the seamline, encasing all raw edges (B). Stitch close to the turned under edge.

For a fast, durable finish, encase the seam allowances in narrow double-fold bias binding (see BIAS TAPES AND BINDINGS). This method is best suited for ruffles applied to the hems of bed or table coverings; it may be too bulky for window treatments, and interfere with the way the treatment drapes.

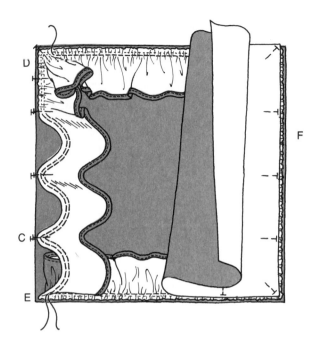

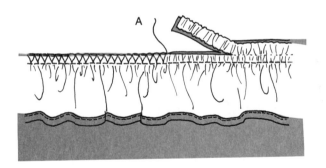

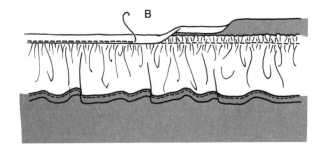

Self-faced Plain Ruffles Self-faced plain ruffles take more fabric, but less time because no hem is needed. They also add a look of quality and, since they're reversible, are a good method for items such as placemats and pillows which have two "right" sides.

Cut self-faced ruffles twice the finished width, plus 1¼" (3.2cm) for seam allowances. Fold in half with *wrong* sides together to create a finished outside edge (A). Gather the raw edges together, and apply, using the techniques for plain ruffles above.

RUFFLES WITH A HEADING

This type of ruffle is gathered off-center to give it a narrow heading, or through the center for a symmetrical double-ruffle effect. It can be used as a top-stitched trim, or as a project edging.

Both long edges of these ruffles need finishing—use narrow hems or double-fold bias binding as described above for plain ruffles, allowing 1¼" (3.2cm) for finishing the edges when cutting. Also as described above, join the two short edges with a French seam if you need to make a continuous ruffle, or narrow hem edges that do not join. Place the rows of long machine stitches for gathering ¼" (6mm) apart. Pin mark both ruffle and project to distribute the gathers evenly, then place the *wrong side* of the ruffle on the *right side* of the project. Pull the bobbin threads to gather the ruffle evenly and pin baste.

Applying to an Edge Finish the project edge with a narrow hem (see HEMS). Topstitch the ruffle over the hem (A).

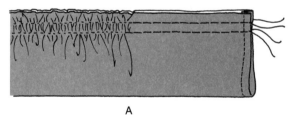

A

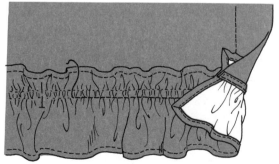

A

Applying away from an Edge
To use headed ruffles as a trim away from a project edge, top-stitch next to each row of gathers (A). Or stitch through the center of the gathering stitches to apply the ruffle with a single stitching.

Self-faced Ruffle with a Heading Like plain ruffles, ruffles with a heading can be self-faced, eliminating the need for hems and making them reversible. Cut the strip twice the finished width of the ruffle. Narrow hem the short ends. Fold with wrong sides together so the raw edges meet on the underside of the ruffle where the gathering stitches will be placed. Where the edges meet, stitch two rows of gathering stitches ¼" (6mm) apart, so each row holds one raw edge in place (A). Topstitch the ruffle to the project, stitching next to the gathering stitches.

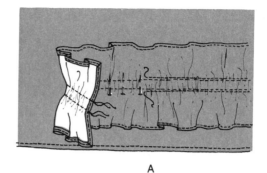

A

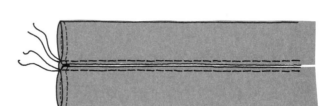

A

Seams

For any home decorating project, it's ideal to work with one seamless expanse of fabric. However, seams are a fact of life. Large projects invariably need piecing, either to create a swath of fabric large enough for the purpose or to use the fabric with a minimum of waste.

Sometimes a plain seam—straight stitched, with the seam allowances pressed open—will work, but more often one of the special seams described below works better. All feature seam allowances pressed to one side, a construction technique which makes seams inherently stronger. Some of the seams are designed to finish raw edges quickly and durably, while others suit certain fabrics best. For professional results with any type of seam, pay extra attention to the information on planning where the seams belong.

WHERE TO SEAM

Unless the seams are to be trimmed or otherwise accented, place them where they'll be noticed the least. It's easy to conceal seams inside pleats, for example, or to adjust gathers so seams fall in a fold rather than to the outside. If you can locate seams on the side or the back of a project and leave the front view unbroken by seams, so much the better.

It's important to cut fabric so the seams are placed symmetrically on curtain panels (A). This helps the fabric to hang the same way on both sides of the window.

A

For bed and table coverings, split the fabric so one full-width panel runs through the center, with equal, partial-width panels on each side (B). This creates a more balanced look than you'd achieve with a single, central seam.

TRIMMING AND GRADING SEAMS

Perfect seams owe as much to trimming and grading the seam allowances as they do to expert stitching. This is true especially for home decorating projects where fabrics tend to be heavy and inserted trims multiply the layers of fabric in a seam.

Trim seam allowances that are turned together in one direction to graduated widths (C). This blends the thickness of the seam allowances so a bulky ridge doesn't show on the right side. Grade the seam allowance layers so the seam allowance next to the right side of the project is the widest.

At a corner, trim across the point, then trim diagonally along both sides of the point (D).

Notch out the seam allowances on outside curves (E). Clip into the seam allowances on inside curves (F).

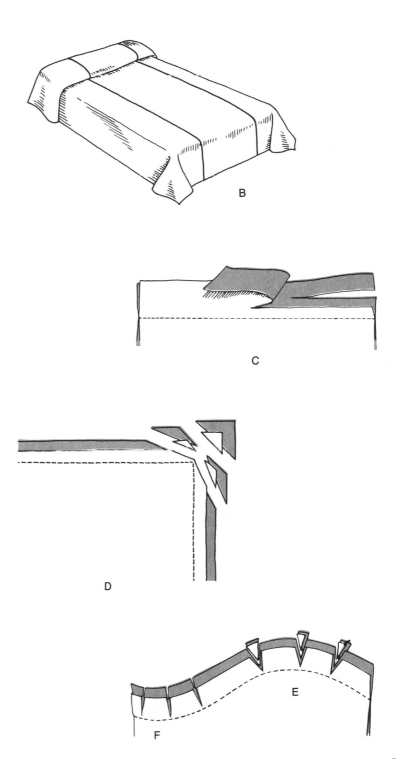

TAPING SEAMS

Twill tape or woven seam binding can be used to reinforce seams and prevent stretching. Just include the tape as you stitch the seam (G).

FINISHING RAW EDGES

Unless you adopt one of the special-purpose seams below, you may want to finish the raw edges of the seam allowances to prevent raveling, for neatness, and for durability.

For fabrics that ravel easily, reinforce the raw edges with zigzag stitches (H), or encase the raw edges with double-fold bias binding (see BIAS TAPES AND BINDINGS).

Lightweight fabrics can be finished by turning under the raw edge and stitching close to the fold (I).

For firmly woven fabrics, stitch ¼″ (6mm) from the edge, then trim with pinking shears (J).

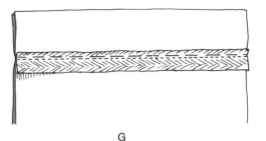

G

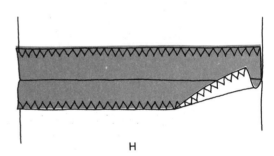

H

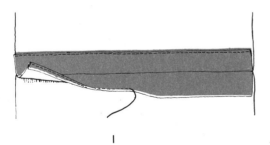

I

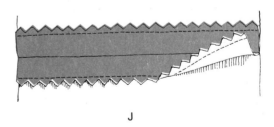

J

Lined rod-pocket curtains, page 93, with basic tiebacks, page 95 (above).

Basic rod-pocket curtains, page 90 (left).

Sash curtains, page 97, with basic roller shade, page 118 (above).

Balloon curtain, page 98 (above).

Pillow with headed ruffle, page 165 (above).

Rod-pocket curtains with ruffles, page 101 (bottom left).

Basic roller shade, page 118 (bottom left).

Shower curtain, page 110 (above).

Ruffled curtains with valance, page 104 (right).

Tab-top curtains with loops and scallops, page 107 (below).

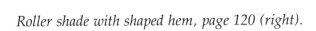

Swag, page 113 (left).

Basic rod-pocket curtains, page 90 (left).

Pillow with ribbon trim, page 163 (left).

Roller shade with shaped hem, page 120 (right).

Roman shade, page 123 (above).

Austrian shade, page 126 (above).

Pillow cover with Turkish corners, page 176 (bottom left).

Balloon shade, page 130 (bottom left).

Basic knife-edge pillow covers, page 161 (left).

Basic throw coverlet, page 136, with gathered dust ruffle, page 153, and pillow sham with flanged edge, page 170 (below).

Eyelet-trimmed throw coverlet, page 138.

Fitted coverlet with pleats, page 143, with box-pleated dust ruffle, page 156 (above).

Basic comforter, page 146, with gathered dust ruffle, page 153 (right).

Fitted coverlet with flounce, page 140, with gathered dust ruffle, page 153.

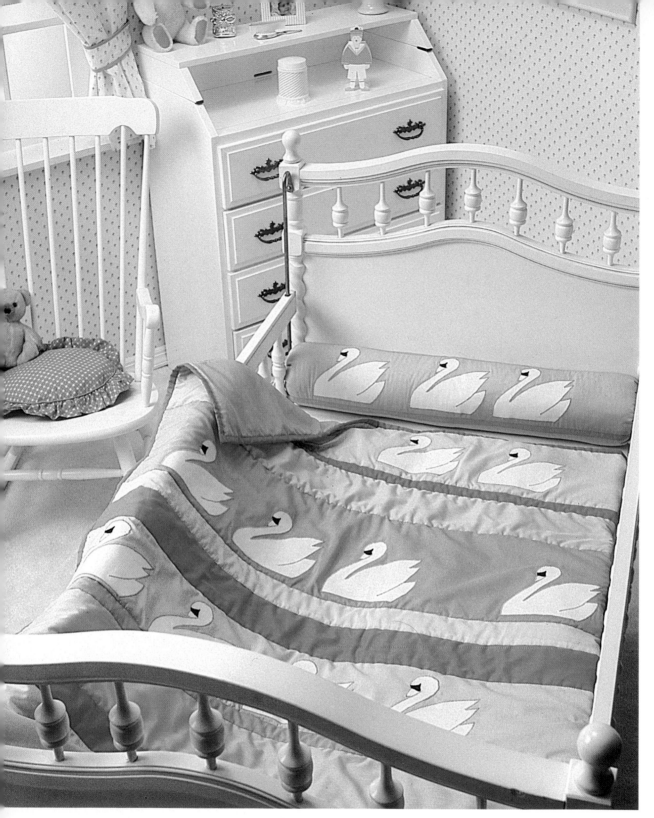

Pieced crib quilt with swan appliqué, page 150.

Pillow cover with headed ruffle, page 165 (above).

Tie-on pillow covers, page 168 (right).

Pillow cover with ribbon trim, page 163 (bottom right).

Pillow cover with welting trim, page 163 (bottom right).

Pillow sham with flanged edge, page 170 (above).

Floor cushions, page 172 (left).

Tufted pillows, page 166 (above).

Bolster pillows with duffle covers, page 174 (above).

Pillow cover with Turkish corners and welting, page 177 (left).

Basic round tablecloth with bias binding, page 181 (top left).

Basic square tablecloth with bias binding, page 185 (top left).

Round tablecloth with ruffle, page 183 (below).

Square tablecloth with ruffle, page 185 (below).

Basic round tablecloths with bias binding, page 181 (above).

Basic oval tablecloth with bias binding, page 184.

Round tablecloth with shirred welting, page 182.

Square tablecloth with plain hem, page 185.

SPECIAL PURPOSE SEAMS

French Seam The classic seam for sheers, this method works best when seams are straight. Two lines of stitching make this narrow, self-finishing seam.

First, pin *wrong* sides together and stitch a ⅜" (10mm) seam (K). Trim the seam allowances to a scant ¼" (6mm).

Then, with right sides together, crease along the seam and press. Stitch a ¼" (6mm) seam, encasing the raw edges (L). Press the seam to one side.

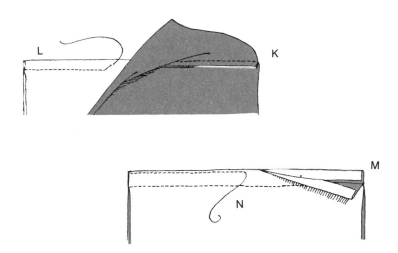

Mock French Seam In place of the French seam, use this adapted method for greater control when matching fabric prints, or for curved seams.

Stitch a plain seam, turn the raw edges in toward each other ¼" (6mm), and press (M). Stitch the folds together close to the edge (N). Press the seam to one side.

Interlocking Seam Professionals use this seam to join panels of fabric for full-length curtains, although it suits any project where you want to enclose the raw edges on a straight seam. Use this method only on light- to mediumweight fabrics. Efficient because it takes just one line of stitching, this seam requires half of the panels to be cut with extra-wide seam allowances, and the other half with narrow seam allowances.

Allow ½" (13mm) seam allowances on one panel, and ¾" (20mm) on the adjoining panel. Right sides together, line up the seamlines of both panels so the larger seam allowance is on

the bottom (O). Fold the bottom seam allowance over the raw edge of the upper panel, and press (P). Make a second fold the same depth and press (Q). Stitch close to the inner fold (R).

Twice-stitched Seam This is another seam suitable for sheers, but it's by no means limited to them. A versatile seam, use it whenever you need to finish raw edges in the least bulky fashion.

Stitch a plain seam. Use a

straight stitch or a zigzag stitch to sew the seam allowances together, ⅛" to ¼" (3 to 6mm) away (S). Trim the seam allowances close to the second stitching, and press the seam allowances to one side.

If your sewing machine can make an overedge stitch (which sews the seam as it overcasts the raw edges), use it to create a twice-stitched seam in a single pass. Trim the seam allowances beforehand.

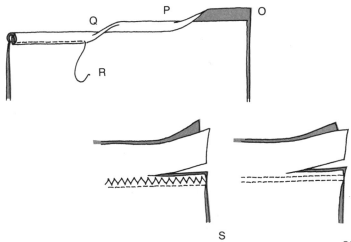

Templates

When sewing any shape in multiple amounts, a sturdy pattern called a template guarantees uniformity. Templates are useful aids when making rounded corners, a set of matching appliqués, or scalloped hems and headings, for example.

MAKING TEMPLATES

Drawing Draw the shape on a stiff material such as extra-fine sandpaper, which makes a non-slip template, or cardboard. Clear plastic or stencil paper from an art supply store can also be used—these have a see-through quality which helps if fabric designs must be carefully positioned for cutting.

Plates, cups, or other round objects can be used to draw curves and scallops; use a ruler to draw straight lines. To copy an illustration for a template, trace the illustration, cut it out, and paste it to the template material. A photocopy can't be used for this, because photocopying changes the size and shape of the original slightly.

Cutting Cut out the template with scissors or, for greater accuracy with complex shapes, use a single-edge razor blade or an X-acto® knife. As they're used, templates wear down around the edges. It's a good idea to cut several templates of the same shape at the beginning of a large project so you can discard worn templates as you work.

USING TEMPLATES

Trace around the template to mark the fabric for cutting. Add seam allowances by eye as you cut, or make a second template with seam allowances included to mark a cutting line. Mark the fabric on the wrong side to use the tracing also as a precise stitching guide; remember to turn the template over so the right side of the fabric has the template design headed in the proper direction.

Templates can also be used as pressing aids. Position the template on the cut-out section, and press the seam allowances over the template edge. In a similar way, you can use a template to preshape bias binding for easier application.

Easy Scallops with a Template

Scalloped edges on curtains, table and bed coverings, or pillows may look complicated, but they're actually easy to design. Begin with a round template, and cut notches to mark the depth of the scallop (A). Draw a straight line across the project edge, or on a piece of paper if you prefer to make a pattern first. Line up the notches on your template with the straight line, and draw the first scallop in the center (B).

Draw the scallop below the line for a curtain heading, or above the line for a scalloped hem. Draw the rest of the scallops an equal distance apart from the center to the ends (C). If the points of the scallops at the ends are a little wider or narrower than those in between, this will hardly be noticeable. Because you've spaced the scallops equally from the center, the entire edge will look balanced.

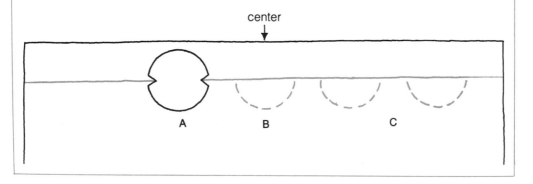

Ties, Drawstrings, and Loops

With these quick methods, you can make finished fabric strips for a number of practical applications. Foremost among their uses when sewing for the home are as budget-minded tab and tie-on headings for window treatments and shower curtains—no hooks or special tapes have to be purchased.

TIES

For each tie, cut a strip on the lengthwise or crosswise grain, whichever uses your fabric with less waste. Cut the strip four times the desired finished width, and add ¼″ (6mm) to the desired finished length.

Wrong sides together, fold the tie in half along its length and press (A). Open up the tie, and fold in one short raw edge ¼″ (6mm) (B). Turn in the two long raw edges to meet the pressed-in lengthwise fold, then bring the two long folds together (C). Stitch the folds together close to the long edge, and across the folded short end (D).

Position the unfinished short end of the tie so it is inserted in a seam.

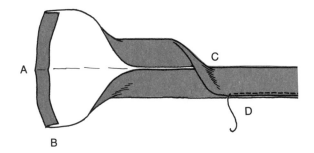

DRAWSTRINGS

Make drawstrings like ties, above, except add ½" (13mm) to the length when cutting. Fold under both short ends ¼" (6mm) before stitching.

LOOPS

Cut a fabric strip long enough for all the loops needed for a project, and four times the desired finished width. Fold under the long raw edges as described above for ties. Omit turning under one short raw edge. Stitch close to both long edges, and cut into equal segments (A). Fold each segment in half to make a loop. Pin or baste across the raw edges (B). Position the raw edges of each loop so they are inserted in a seam of a project.

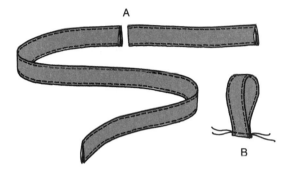

Trims

Most home decorating projects are simple in style, so when you feel "something's missing," think about adding some trim. Add a little bit to accent seams or introduce a spot of color, or use trims lavishly to decorate edges and coordinate several different items in a room. In addition to the band and lace trims included here, fabric trims such as RUFFLES, WELTING, and BIAS TAPES AND BINDING can be used to add interest and dressmaker details to home decorating projects.

BAND TRIMS

These trims have two finished edges, and include braids, ribbons, and single-fold bias tape. Flat eyelet trims and galloon lace with two bordered edges, as well as beading, also belong in this group.

Applying Pin, baste, or use a glue stick to hold these trims in place, then stitch close to both long edges to apply them. Or use fusible web (see FUSING TECHNIQUES) for a quick, iron-on application with flat braid or ribbon trims.

Very narrow band trims can be zigzag stitched in place. Use a medium to long stitch length, encasing the trim edges as the needle swings from side to side.

Joining Ends Plan ahead so the ends meet at an inconspicuous place on your project. On thick trims, cut the ends so they butt. Whipstitch the ends or coat them lightly with clear-drying glue to prevent ravels. Whipstitch (see HAND STITCHES) the edges together (A).

On nonbulky trims, fold under one raw edge and lap it over the other (B). Slipstitch the fold if desired.

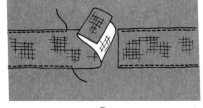

B

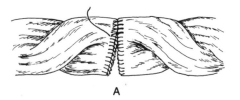

A

Mitering Corners Use this simple miter to shape the trim squarely at a corner.

Stitch close to the inner edge of the trim, to the corner. Fold the trim back on itself, then fold the trim down to turn the corner. Finger press the diagonal fold at the corner, then lift up the trim to stitch on the diagonal crease (C). Trim away the triangle below the stitching if using a lace or thick trim. Finish by edgestitching the trim.

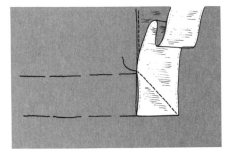

C

LACE EDGINGS

Lace edgings have one raw edge and one finished edge. On some laces, such as eyelet trims, the raw edge is scalloped; trim edge straight before applying.

Applying Use narrow French seams (see SEAMS) to apply lace to an edge. To insert lace edging in a seam, baste the lace to the seamline with right sides together, before stitching the seam.

Joining Ends Use a narrow French or twice-stitched seam (see SEAMS) to join the ends of lace edgings.

Mitering Corners Use a simple miter, as described earlier for band trims. For a softer corner, gather the lace at the corner to provide enough extra edging for the trim to lay flat without cupping.

Tying Quilts and Comforters

Tying layers of fabric and filler together is often thought of as a quick alternative to quilting, but tying rightfully deserves a niche all its own in home decorating. It's the method of choice when you want to create a lush, deeply padded comforter with high-loft batting, or when using multiple layers of batting for a custom overstuffed effect.

PREPARING TO TIE

Marking Fold the quilt or comforter top lengthwise and then crosswise to find the center. Using tailor's chalk or water erasable marker, mark a dot in the center on the right side. Working out to the edges from this central point, mark the entire top at each spot where the piece will be tied. Stop marking about 4" (10cm) from the edges, to leave an untied border.

Tying designs such as staggered rows or parallel rows are popular, but many others can be used. You may prefer to arrange the ties to echo a fabric motif or space them to accent seams or appliqués. If you are using a stable polyester batting, tying approximately every 6" to 12" (15 to 30.5cm) anchors the filler successfully for laundering.

Assembling the Layers Baste the top, filler, and backing together with lines of stitches radiating out to the edges from the center (see QUILTING BY MACHINE), or as directed for your specific project.

TYING TECHNIQUES

With all of the tying methods given below, begin at the center of the project and work toward the edges. Wait until all the tying threads or ribbons have been inserted to begin making the knots.

Tufts For each tie, thread a needle with 12″ (30.5cm) of perle cotton or six-strand embroidery floss. Work with the thread doubled, so the working length is 6″ (15cm).

Working from the top, insert the needle ½″ (13mm) alongside the mark, through all thicknesses (A). Bring the needle up from the backing side ½″ (13mm) on the other side of the mark (B).

To finish, make sure the tie ends are even, pull them tightly, and make square knots (C). This draws up the fabric to form a small pleat under each tie for a soft, deep padding. If you don't want a small pleat, make the stitches closer together. Trim the tie ends (D), and separate the thread strands to form tufts (E).

Tack Quilting For this method, mark the quilt or comforter backing, and tie from the backing side. Thread the needle with 16″ (41cm) lengths of perle cotton doubled through the needle, so the working length is 8″ (20.5cm).

Working from the backing, insert the needle at the mark, through all thicknesses (A). Then insert the needle ¼″ (6mm) alongside the mark from the top, through all thicknesses (B). Insert the needle at the original mark, through all thicknesses, then from the top as before (C). To finish, tie square knots and trim the perle cotton ends evenly (D).

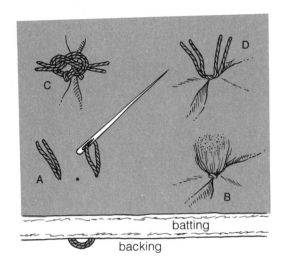

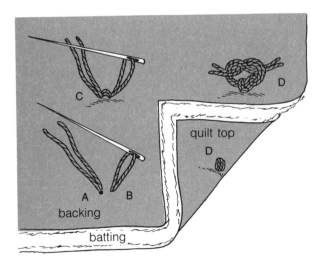

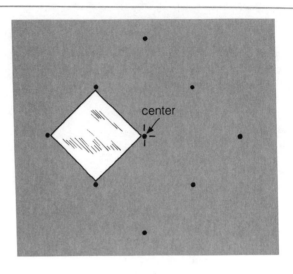

center

Mark a Top Quickly for Tying

Use a square cardboard template to make equally spaced marks for tying. For staggered rows, place the template diagonally, beginning at the center. To mark straight rows, place the template parallel to the edge of the top.

Ribbon Bows There are two ways to decorate a tied quilt or comforter with ribbon bows.

Narrow ribbon, in the ⅛″ (3mm) or ¹⁄₁₆″ (2mm) width, can be used instead of perle cotton or floss for tying. Adapt the tufting method given above by using a 12″ (30.5cm) length of ribbon in the needle, and do not double it. After knotting, use the ends of the ribbon to tie a bow. Trim the ribbon ends diagonally.

Any ribbon width can be tied into bows, then sewed by hand to the knots of perle cotton or floss tufts. Use 12″ (30.5cm) lengths of ribbon for the bows, and trim the ends diagonally after sewing them in place.

Welting

Welting is fabric-covered cord, a distinctive detail for many home decorating projects. Inserted in the seams of a pillow, welting makes a smart, tailored edging. Around the edge of a chair cushion, the welting takes the wear and tear the cover itself would otherwise suffer and makes the seams stronger. Add it to a floor-length table covering to encourage a graceful flare at the hem, or use it in the seams of a bedspread for a custom accent.

Cable cord and soft piping cord are used as the fillers, which is why welting is often called "cording" or "piping." Decorators sometimes use jumbo cord for an emphatically large welting, or shirr the fabric covering for a luxurious dressmaker detail—ideas which are easy to copy at home. Welting also can be purchased ready-made in solid colors, with either fine or medium cord as the filler.

MAKING WELTING

Cutting the Bias Covering Cut and piece the bias strips using the method for making BIAS TAPES AND BINDINGS. To figure how wide the strips should be, pin a bias scrap of your fabric around the cord so it fits snugly. Open up the scrap to measure the amount needed to encase the cord, then add 1¼" (3.2cm) for seam allowances, and ¼" to ⅜" (6mm to 10mm) for removing the slack.

Stitching the Covering Fold the bias strip over the cord so the raw fabric edges meet with wrong sides together (A). With a zipper foot on your machine, stitch close to the cord (B). Use a fairly long, straight stitch and position the stitches so the fabric fits the cord snugly without squeezing it; another row of stitches will be added later between this stitching and the cord. Because the bias cut makes the fabric so pliant, it's important to stretch the bias strip as you sew. This removes the slack and molds the fabric to the cord for a beautifully smooth welting.

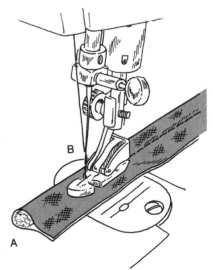

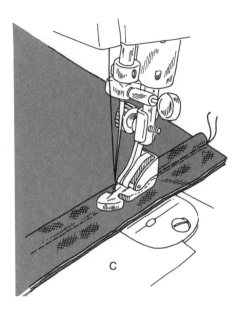

C

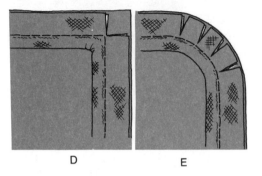

D   E

APPLYING WELTING

Two stitchings are needed to apply welting. First, machine baste the welting to the seamline of the project; use a zipper foot to position the basting stitches right next to the welting (C).

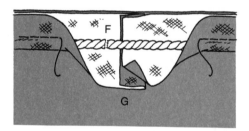

G

To turn a square corner, clip into the welting seam allowance (D).

To round a curve, clip into the welting seam allowance as often as necessary to make the seam allowance lie flat (E).

Where the ends meet, plan ahead by positioning the joining at an inconspicuous place. Leave a small amount of welting free at the beginning and end as you baste. Pick out the stitches to open up the bias covering, and trim the cord so the ends abut (F). Sew the ends together securely. Trim the bias covering for an overlap seam

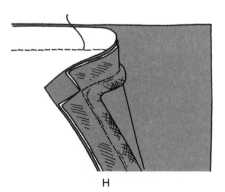

H

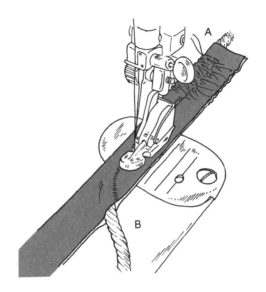

(G), allowing enough fabric to turn under the raw edge ¼" (6mm). Refold the bias covering to finish basting the welting in place.

To finish, place the section with the basted welting on top of the other project section or facing. Sew the seam with a zipper foot, stitching on the seamline (H). Grade the seam allowances to reduce bulk.

MAKING OTHER TYPES OF WELTING

Shirred Welting Make this welting variation by cutting a straight grain fabric strip twice as long as the cord filler. Fold the strip right side out over the cord, with the raw edges even. Use a zipper foot to stitch across the end, through all thicknesses, then pivot at the corner to stitch close to the cord (A). When you have stitched about 6" (15cm), stop stitching. Leave the needle in the fabric. Shirr the stitched portion by pulling the cord toward you while holding the fabric in back of the presser foot (B). Push the stitched portion back toward the end until it is tightly shirred.

Continue stitching and shirring until the cord is fully covered. Baste across the other end of the welting when you've finished to prevent the shirring from shifting. Arrange the shirring evenly along the length of the cord.

Cording This type of welting is unique because the fabric covering is stitched wrong side out around the cord filler, then it's turned right side out over the cord. Instead of using this welting as a seam insertion, slip-stitch it to the right side of a project edge or seam as a finishing touch.

To make cording, cut the cord twice the length of cording needed. Wrap the bias covering strip around the cord, *wrong* side out, beginning in the center of the cord (A). Use a zipper foot to stitch across the cord, through all thicknesses, and

continue stitching 2 to 3 stitches beyond the cord. Then pivot and taper back about 1" (2.5cm) until the stitches are close to the cord (B). This tapering allows the fabric to turn right side out over the cord easily after the stitching is completed. Continue stitching close to the cord, being careful not to catch the cord in the stitching.

To turn the covering to the right side, pull the uncovered cord as you slide the fabric over it (C). Cut off the excess uncovered cord.

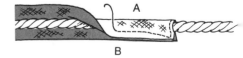

Window Treatments

Dressing your windows is a wonderful way to put your creativity on display. The sewing goes quickly, because most projects require little more than straight seams and hems, but then that's just the beginning. There are so many ways to decorate a basic panel of fabric—with trims, tiebacks, ruffles, and different styles of headings—you're bound to be inspired to go beyond the basics.

In this section, you'll find out how to sew these components of window treatments:

- Curtains with various headings, ruffles, and optional tiebacks.

- Valances and swags, to frame the top of the window, and, if you like, cascade down the sides.

- Shades, including roller, Roman, Austrian, and balloon styles.

Any of these elements can be used alone or combined in countless ways for unique, layered window treatments.

BEGIN WITH THE WINDOW ITSELF

To plan an effective window treatment, it's a good idea to think about how your windows operate. There are many exciting alternatives for dressing windows, no matter what their size or shape, so make a choice which allows the window to function without interference. A summary of the kinds of rods and other supporting hardware which are available for specific kinds of window treatments can be found on the following pages. If you're facing problem windows, there's probably a rod or bracket mentioned there to help.

One common window type has two sashes which slide up and down and is called a *double-hung window*. These windows can be dressed many different ways, using just a valance or a simple shade for a minimal approach, or with full-length curtains over sheers plus a draped swag for a more formal feeling. Few window treatments will interfere with the window's operation.

Sliding windows, including sliding glass doors, have panels of glass which move back and forth in metal or wooden tracks. Rods or shade brackets can be mounted inside or outside window frames, but mount hardware outside the frame of doors so shades can be raised clear of the opening.

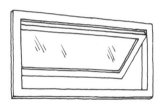

Jalousie, awning, and casement windows that open outward present few limits for window treatments as long as the arrangement does not block easy access to the crank or handle used to open the window.

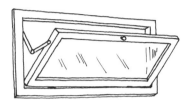

Hopper and casement windows that open inward require special window treatments. Tab-top curtains which can be pulled back to stack clear of the window, or shades mounted high enough over the frame so they can be raised above the window, are most practical in this situation. Curtains can also be installed on the window itself, with a rod at the top and the bottom of the curtain to hold it securely in place.

Stationary windows in doors can be treated most simply with a curtain, shirred top and bottom onto a rod. A shade or valance, or both, are alternatives, especially if you want to echo window treatments used elsewhere in the room.

OTHER PRACTICAL MATTERS

Besides planning a window treatment which allows easy operation of the window, there are a few other practical matters to think about. Do you want to frame an attractive view, or cover up the glass to hide what you see? Can you show off beautiful windows with a minimal treatment, or do you need to cover them up for privacy's sake? If conserving energy is one of your priorities, think about using closely fitted shades that block drafts, thermal curtain linings, or layered window treatments, which insulate effectively because they trap air between the multiple fabric panels. Whatever your needs, you can devise a window treatment to meet them.

CREATIVE STRATEGIES

If your windows are less than perfect in size and placement, consider how a window treatment can make them look more pleasing:

- To make windows look taller, hang full-length curtains above the window frame, and use sheer panels underneath to conceal the actual height of the window. You can also add a deep valance which begins above the frame and covers its top.

- To make windows look wider, extend the window treatment beyond the frame on both sides. A gracefully draped swag can add a horizontal accent to create a wider appearance too, as can tiers of tab-top curtains.

- Small, insignificant windows gain importance with treatments which make them focal points. Use a boldly patterned fabric, an intriguing valance or swag, puffy balloon shades, or lushly ruffled curtains to compensate for windows that lack impact on their own. Small hopper windows, which usually are located awkwardly near the ceiling, can be draped in tiers of tab-top curtains which extend all the way to the floor.

- Poorly placed windows almost disappear when they're dressed simply in a fabric which matches the wall. Plain roller shades are a good choice for this.

- Windows of different sizes in a room can be treated alike for a more balanced look. Begin with the largest window to determine where to place the rods or other supporting hardware, and install the rest to match.

INSTALLING WINDOW TREATMENTS

Whether you're making curtains, swags, fabric shades, or a layered window treatment which combines several of these, you'll need to install the rod or other supporting hardware first so you can measure accurately to estimate how much fabric you'll need. Selecting these items can be a real adventure, because there's so much to choose from. Curtain rods have become fashionable room accessories, for example, and there's a choice of many decorative styles as well as the conventional types. An attractive rod might give you an idea for an inventive window treatment, so it's a tossup as to which comes first—the hardware or deciding which kind of window treatment to make.

In any case, the rod or other supports should be an early purchase. For many projects, you'll need additional supplies such as special tapes, cords, and backings. How-to's for window treatments begin on page 91, and the specific materials needed are presented at the start of each project category for your use as a shopping guide.

Tools for Installing Window Treatments These tools are generally useful to a household as well as helpful for installing window treatments. If you prefer not to purchase the power tools, look into the possibility of renting them:

- Drill—to install screws for brackets which support rods and shades. Power drills are fast and easy to use, but hand-operated drills are less expensive. Regardless of which you choose, always use drills with extreme care. You'll need a selection of drill bits. For each hole, you'll need a bit to drill a hole slightly smaller than the screw.

- Level—to be sure rods and brackets are installed straight. A carpenter's level is ideal.

- Saw—to cut window-shade rollers and mounting boards. A small handsaw will do the job.

- Staple gun or hammer—to attach hook and loop tape to shade mounting boards. Electric staple guns are fast and easy to use. Manual staple guns require more strength to operate, but are less expensive. Instead of a staple gun, you can use flat-headed tacks and a hammer.

Curtains

Depending upon your choice of fabric and trim, the curtains you sew can create an informal or formal mood in a room. Informal curtains are usually made from light- to mediumweight fabrics such as voile, dotted Swiss, gingham, muslin, homespun, and open weaves. Among the possible trims are ruffles, contrasting bias binding, braid, and fringe. For a more formal feeling, make your curtains from medium to heavier weight fabrics such as sateen, chintz, antique satin, wool flannel, raw silk, and linen weaves, or select a beautiful bordered lace. Lustrous ribbons and elaborate upholstery braids make suitable edgings, and there's always the option of adding a lining to help your curtain drape in elegant, luxurious folds.

HARDWARE, SUPPLIES, AND NOTIONS FOR CURTAINS

Curtain rods are easy to select because there are just a few basic types. The best one for your project depends upon whether you want the curtain to hang right next to the glass or not.

Projecting Rods These rods have elbow bends at the corners and extend out from the mounting surface (A). Mount them on the wall to make a window look taller and/or wider, or on the outer corners of the window frame so the curtains completely cover the window. Sew rod-pocket headings (B) to hang the curtains. A set of brackets (C) is needed for each rod, plus screws to install the brackets.

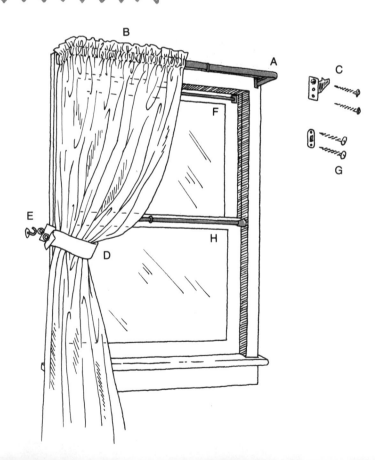

Rods with projections from 1¼" to 4" (3.2 to 10cm) are available. Choose a projection which allows the curtains to hang clear of the baseboard moldings, window sill, and any radiators, air conditioners, or similar units.

Special Projecting Rods Rods for valances, which hang over curtains at the top of the window, project even further—standard clearances include 6¼" (15.8cm), 7½" (19cm), and 8¼" (21cm). There are double rods for hanging two sets of curtains; use these also to hang crisscross tieback curtains or a valance over curtains.

A continental rod is a type of projecting rod which is 4½" (11.5cm) deep. When slipped into the curtain heading, it creates the effect of a shirred valance. Unusual rods for curved, corner, and bay windows are also available. These may not be stocked but can be ordered through many stores.

Tiebacks If you want to make fabric tiebacks for your curtains, you'll need 4 small plastic rings (D) and 2 cup hooks (E) for each pair of tiebacks. Decorative tieback hooks are also available as alternatives to plain cup hooks.

Sash Rods Sash rods (F) are used to hang curtains next to the window frame or on a door. The standard sash rod is flat, painted metal, but there are also round, brass sash rods for sheer curtains. Usually a set of brackets (G), plus screws to install the brackets, is needed for

each rod, but some sash rods have the bracket built into the ends of the rod itself so the curtain can be hung flush with the mounting surface.

Tension rods (H) are a type of sash rod which requires no brackets or screws. These rods are held in place by a hidden spring, and are ideal wherever drilling holes is impractical Special strong, rustproof tension rods are available for shower curtains.

Pole Rods Pole rods (I) can be used for either rod-pocket curtains, or tab-top curtains which have open headings with loops or rings. These rods are decorative as well as functional, and are available in wood, brass,

---

Tips for Installing Curtain Rods

The installation of your curtain rods is so important to the success of a window treatment, you'll want to do it carefully:

- Don't assume all windows in a room are the same, even if they look alike. Measure and install rods for each window on an individual basis. Use a folding ruler or a steel tape measure for accuracy.

- Window moldings, floors, and ceilings can be off-square, or on a slant, even in new homes. Don't depend on them as frames of reference—use a carpenter's level to make sure rods are installed straight. Rods support the curtain or drapery fabric, and they must be level for the fabric to drape evenly.

- Make sure brackets are installed securely. Screws are fine for installing brackets on wood, but they won't do the job on plaster or hollow gypsum board (wall board) walls. Use expansion bolts or toggle bolts which have spreading anchors. On brick and concrete surfaces, use masonry

bolts with expanding plastic plugs. On aluminum or steel window frames, use self-drilling screws called drivers; lubricate drivers with a bar of soap for easier installation.

- For long rods, or rods which will support heavy curtains, an extra bracket called an intermediate support keeps the rod from sagging. Intermediate supports are available for all types of rods; you'll need one about every 4 feet (12.2 meters).

- Installing rods for tab-top or café curtains requires preplanning. First, you must decide how many tiers you're going to make. Most windows look best with two or three tiers—divide the window into halves or thirds to install the rods. If you are dressing multi-paned windows, line up the rods with the mullions (the moldings which separate the glass panes) for a professional look. The tiers don't have to be equal; in fact, a longer tier on the bottom can make a window treatment look more balanced than when all the tiers are the same size.

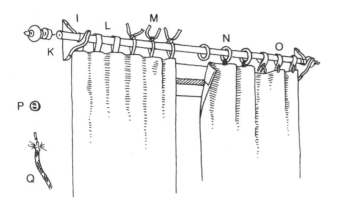

and painted metal to suit different decorating schemes. Finials (J)—decorative tips—for the ends of pole rods may be included with the rod, or purchased separately in various styles, depending upon the kind of rod you've selected. A pair of decorative brackets (K) is needed for each rod, plus screws for installing the brackets.

Tab-top Headings for Pole Rods Tab-top curtains have a heading which exposes the rod. You can sew tab headings with loops (L) or ties (M). Or use sew-on rings (N) or clip-on rings (O).

Linings If you choose to line your window treatment, investigate the many different kinds of fabrics available. Some linings have flame-retardant, water-repellent, or crease-resistant properties, for example, in addition to offering protection from fading and sun-rot. There are linings which are insulated to make them superb sound barriers, and linings with reflective backings for the ultimate in energy conservation.

There are also "dimout" linings to darken rooms, as well as "blackout" linings which are laminated to vinyl for complete light blockage. A local fabric shop may have to order these for you. Cotton sateen is a traditional lining which is widely available, or you could easily improvise by using sheets or muslin.

The fiber content of most linings is 100 percent cotton or 50 percent cotton/50 percent polyester, and usually they can be washed or dry-cleaned. However, some specialty linings are made from rayon or acetate alone and require a specific kind of care. Check the care requirements of the lining to be sure they're compatible with other fabrics used for the window treatment.

Most linings are 48" (122cm) wide, but some are a little narrower. Some are extra-wide—up to 115" (292.5cm). When your window treatment is installed, lining seams can show through as shadows; if you can match the lining and window treatment fabric widths, the seams will line up attractively on both layers. If you use an ex-

tra-wide lining fabric, it may be possible to cut a seamless lining without concern for seam show-through—this saves sewing time, too.

Lining color can affect the appearance of your window treatment, so hold both the outer fabric and the lining together up to the sunlight when you make your selection. For linings, you'll usually have a choice of white, plus ivory or natural. If you want to present a uniform look to passers-by, use the same lining color for all your window treatments.

Weights As a finishing touch, add sew-on drapery weights to the hem (P) at corners and seams. For full-length sheers, there are covered chain weights (Q) which slip into the hem fold.

MEASURING TO ESTIMATE FABRIC

Always install the rods first, then take your measurements for curtains. Use a steel measuring tape or folding ruler for accuracy, and measure each window individually, even if you are making matching treatments. All the windows in a room may not be identical.

The measurements you take are just the starting point. It's important to understand that, at this stage, you're measuring the *finished length*—the length your curtains will be when they're fully sewn. To find the *total length*—how long to cut each curtain panel—you must add allowances for hems and headings.

For the curtain width, you're

measuring the *raw width*—the width of the curtain panels after they've been installed. To find the *finished width*, you'll need to add an allowance for fabric fullness. To find the *total width*—how wide to cut each curtain panel—you must add allowances for side hems and panel seams.

This helps you estimate basic fabric requirements as well as guides you when cutting the fabric. To arrive at the total fabric estimate, you'll also have to allow fabric for details such as ruffles and tiebacks, and extra fabric for matching prints, stripes, or plaids.

After determining the finished length and finished width for the curtains, use the worksheet and formulas below to estimate how much fabric you'll need. They're set up to make sure you can't forget anything.

As a final precutting step, use graph paper to devise a cutting plan. Mark off the full width of your fabric on the graph, then draw in the measurements of the individual rectangles of fabric which you'll need to cut.

Finished Length For rod-pocket curtains, begin to measure the finished length from the top of the rod or pole (A, B, C). If using café rings or tabs at the heading of your curtain, place a ring on the rod or decide the length of the tabs to help you determine where the finished edge should hang (D). Begin to measure from this edge. End this measurement where you want the bottom hem to fall—usually this is at the sill, the apron, or the floor. For floor-

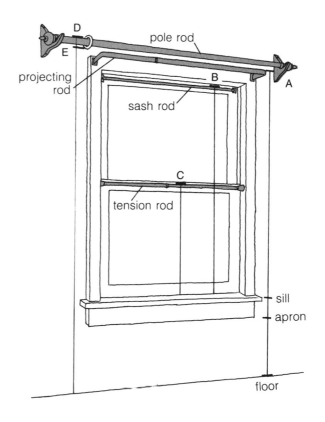

length styles, plan to place the bottom hem high enough to clear carpeting or baseboard heating ducts, or plan for extra-long panels that drift luxuriously on the floor.

Finished Width The width measurement you'll take is actually a raw measurement. For the *raw width*, measure across sash, tension or pole rods. As you measure across projecting rods, include the returns (the distance from the wall to the bend in the rod) in the raw width. To determine the *finished width*, multiply the raw width by 2 for standard fabric fullness, or by 2½ for a fuller, lush look. Multiply by 3 if you're using a sheer fabric. Lace and tab-top curtains usually have minimal fullness, so multiply the raw width by 1½ in these cases.

85

Recording Curtain Measurements

Finished length and bottom: To the finished length as you've measured it, add a hem allowance. For curtains, the standard hem allowance is 3″ (7.5cm).

- For plain hems add 3½″ (9cm)
- For double hems add 6″ (15cm)
- If you're adding ruffles to the bottom edge, subtract the depth of the finished ruffle and add ⅝″ (15mm) for a seam allowance.

Casing: To decide how much to add for a casing, pin a tape measure around the rod and note the measurement. The casing should not fit tightly; add extra to allow the casing to slide easily (see CASINGS). Also add twice the depth of a self-ruffle if you want to extend the casing for this detail at the top. Divide the total casing measurement by 2, then add ¼″ to ½″ (6mm to 13mm) for turning under the raw edge.

Finished Length (minus any ruffle) _____

+ Bottom Hem or Seam Allowance _____

+ Casing   _____

Total Length _____

Finished width and side hems:
To the finished width as you've measured it, add side hem and/or seam allowances. The standard side hem allowance is a 1″ (2.5cm) double hem, so allow 2″ (5cm) for each side hem, or a total of 4″ (10cm) for each panel.

- If you're adding ruffles to any side edges, subtract the depth of

the finished ruffle and add a ⅝″ (15mm) seam allowance per edge instead of a hem allowance.

- If you're making a lined curtain, add 3″ (7.5cm) to each panel for side hem and seam allowances instead of a hem allowance.

Finished Width (minus any ruffle) _____

+ Allowance for Side Hems or Seams _____

Total Width _____

Recording Lining Measurements

If lining a rod-pocket curtain, make the following adjustments to the *finished length* and *finished width* measurements of the curtain panel:

Total length: To determine the total length of the lining panel, add 2½" (6.5cm) to the *finished length* of the curtain panel.

Finished Length of Curtain _____

+ 2½" (6.5cm) _____

- - - - - - - -

Total Length of Lining _____

Total width: To determine the total width of the lining, subtract 1" (2.5cm) from the *finished width* of the curtain.

Finished Width of One Curtain Panel _____

− 1" (2.5cm) _____

- - - - - - - -

Total Width of Lining _____

Estimating Fabric for Curtains and Linings

The formulas below are designed to help you estimate how much fabric you'll need, based on the total length and total width of the window treatment. A calculator makes quick work of the math, or you can simply round off all the numbers involved to make the math easier. Just remember to round upward each time, so you'll have plenty of fabric.

1. Find the number of fabric widths needed for the total width of your curtains.

$$\frac{\text{Total Width}}{\text{Fabric Width Minus } 1\frac{1}{4}'' \ (3.2\text{cm}) \text{ for Seams}} = \begin{array}{l}\text{Number of Widths} \\ \text{Needed*}\end{array}$$

*If this number does not come out evenly, you need to make a decision. Usually you don't cut less than one half a panel, so you can round off this number to the next highest (or lowest) whole number and make your curtains more (or less) full.

2. Multiply the number of widths needed by the total length. This gives you a basic fabric estimate.

$$\text{Number of Widths Needed} \times \text{Total Length} = \begin{array}{l}\text{Basic Fabric} \\ \text{Estimate}\end{array}$$

3. *To this basic estimate, add extra fabric* for ruffles (see page 58), tiebacks (see page 95), and facings, loops, or ties for tab-top headings (see page 107). If your fabric is a plaid, stripe, or print, add the length of one design repeat per panel of fabric. The same amount of fabric is needed for fabrics with or without nap, so no extra allowance is necessary for a with-nap cutting plan.

Basic Fabric Estimate   _____

   + Fabric for Ruffles   _____

   + Fabric for Tiebacks   _____

   + Fabric for Tab-top Headings _____

   + Fabric for Matching
       Plaids, Stripes, Prints   _____

—————————————————————

        Total Fabric Needed[†] _____

[†]Divide by 36 (100) to convert this number into yards (meters).

ROD-POCKET CURTAINS

All you need is fabric to make this type of curtain—no hooks, tapes, or stiffeners. The rod pocket is the casing which forms the curtain heading. Insert a projecting, sash, tension, or pole rod into the casing to hang the curtains. To form a decorative self-ruffle above the rod, cut the casing extra wide and use two rows of stitching.

Basic Rod-pocket Curtains One way to use basic rod-pocket curtains is in a layered treatment which hangs from a double curtain rod. Make a set of sheer curtains to hang next to the window. Make the second set of curtains by the same method but from a heavier fabric, then slide them to the ends of the rod. To bridge the gap in the center of the rod, you can make a rod cover from matching fabric.

HOW-TO

1. *Measure the curtain rod and estimate fabric requirements (see pages 85–89). The standard side hem (A) is a 1" (2.5cm) deep, double hem, and the standard bottom hem is a 3" to 4" (7.5 to 10cm) deep, double hem (B). You may prefer to make wider hems on lightweight or sheer fabrics to add extra body to the edges. On heavy or textured fabrics, plain hems can be used for less bulk. Miter the corners of the bottom hem for a quality finish. Hems can also be fused (see FUSING TECHNIQUES).*

Allow extra fabric if you want to make a rod cover. You'll need a crosswise strip of fabric half as long as the curtain rod, and as wide as the curtain casing allowance plus 1¼" (3.2cm) for seams, and an allowance for a self-ruffle, if desired.

2. *Test the fabric for shrinkage and straighten the grain (see CUTTING FABRIC).*

3. *Work on a large, flat surface to mark and cut the fabric. Use a yardstick (meterstick) as a straight edge to help you mark cutting lines for the total length of the first panel. If your fabric is wider than the total width, mark this first panel with cutting lines for the total width as well. If working with a plaid, stripe, or print, be sure to balance the motifs, and if working with a fabric that has a one-way sheen, texture, or design, use a with-nap cutting plan (see CUTTING LAYOUTS).*

Cut out the first panel.

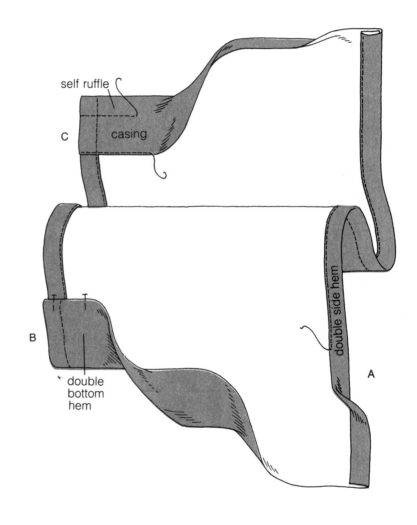

self ruffle

casing

C

double side hem

A

B

double bottom hem

It's a good idea to use this first panel as a trial run. Make the casing heading and the bottom hem on it, using basting stitches so you can remove them easily. Hang the panel up on the rod. You may find the way your fabric drapes requires a change in the measurements, so use this first panel as a master to make adjustments.

Mark and cut out the remaining panels to match the first panel. Align plaids, stripes, and prints to match on all the panels. If you're cutting fabric for more than one window in a room, align the fabric design the same way on all the windows. Remember to match fabric designs at the seams if you must piece together fabric widths for the panels. Mark the position for the casing fold and stitching lines.

4. Trim off the selvages, which are tightly woven and can interfere with the way the fabric drapes.

If it's necessary to seam fabric widths together, use French or interlocking seams (see SEAMS). Use a slightly long stitch of 8–10 per inch (2.5cm) so the seams will not pucker.

5. On each panel, stitch the side hems first, then the bottom hem (see HEMS).

6. For the rod-pocket heading, make a casing with a self-ruffle (see CASINGS) (C).

7. To make the rod cover, narrow hem the short ends of the fabric strip.

Fold the strip in half along its length, right sides together, and stitch the raw edges in a ⅝" (15mm) seam (A). Turn to the right side. Press. To form a self-ruffle, make a line of stitching parallel to the folded edge as sewn on the curtain casing (B).

8. To hang the curtains, insert the rod into the rod cover, then into the casing on each curtain panel. Adjust the curtains so they drape in even folds.

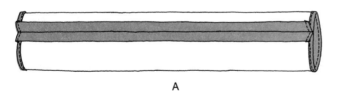

A

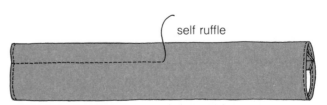

self ruffle

B

Lined Rod-pocket Curtains

Adding a lining is a quality touch for rod-pocket curtains, for they'll hang in richer folds and last longer with this extra fabric backing. There are many functional fabrics available for lining purposes, but you could also use an attractive print or a contrasting solid decorative fabric for subtle detailing.

HOW-TO

1. *Measure the curtain rod and estimate the fabric and lining required (see pages 85–89).*

2. *Test the fabric for shrinkage and straighten the fabric grain (see* CUTTING FABRIC*). Do this both for the curtain fabric and the lining fabric.*

3. *Follow step 3 for the basic rod-pocket curtain above to cut the fabric panels for the curtains and the lining. For lined curtains, the bottom hems are put in first, so it's doubly important to baste together a master panel as a check on your measurements.*

4. *Trim off the selvages, which are tightly woven and can interfere with the way the fabrics drape. If it's necessary to seam fabric widths together for the curtain or the lining, use plain seams and press them open. Use a slightly long machine stitch of 8–10 stitches per inch so the seams do not pucker.*

5. *Make a 3" (7.5cm) double bottom hem on the curtain panel, and a 3" (7.5cm) plain hem on the lining panel (see* HEMS*).*

6. *Place the lining on the curtain panel, right sides together, so the bottom edge of the lining hem is*

93

1" (2.5cm) above the bottom edge of the curtain, and so one side edge of the curtain and lining match (A). (Lining should extend into casing area.) Sew this side seam, using a ½" (13mm) seam allowance (B).

Slide the lining over so it lines up with the curtain edge to sew the other side seam (C). Press the seams toward the lining.

7. Turn the lining right side out. Center the lining so two 1" (2.5cm) hems of curtain fabric form at each side (D). Press the hems at the sides of the curtain. Pin the upper edge of lining in place. Finish the bottom edges of

the hems by mitering the corners (E).

Fold under the top edge of the curtain ¼" to ½" (6 to 13mm) (F).

8. For the rod-pocket heading, make a casing with a self-ruffle (see CASINGS).

9. Link the lining hem to the curtain panel with swing tacks at the seams, or every few feet (30.5cm) (see HAND STITCHES). This helps the two layers of fabric to blend together into identical folds as they hang from the rod.

10. To hang the curtains, insert the rod into the casing and adjust the fabric into even folds.

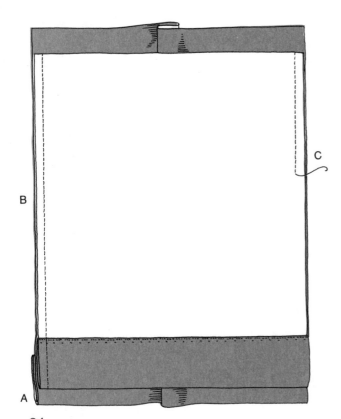

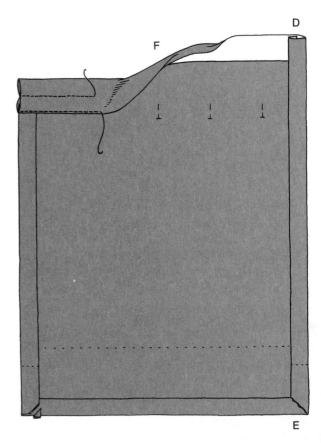

Basic Tiebacks A pair of tiebacks is often used to pull rod-pocket curtains to the sides of a window, making the curtains a graceful frame for what's underneath—that might be another set of curtains, a fabric shade, or just a pleasant outdoor view. Since tiebacks are simple strips of fabric, they're perfect candidates for creative decorations. Add ribbon, lace, fringe, braid, or ruffles to trim them to match your curtains, for example. Or quilt them, appliqué them, or cut them from fabric which is left over from other room projects such as cushions or table coverings for a custom accent. In addition to fabric, you'll need fusible interfacing, a pair of cup hooks, and 4 small plastic rings for each pair of tiebacks. If you prefer a softer look, you can omit the interfacing.

HOW-TO

1. *Tiebacks that are a standard finished size of 4" × 18" (10 × 46cm) require about ¼ yd (0.25m) of fabric and two 4" × 18" (10 × 46cm) strips of fusible interfacing.*

Test the length and width of these tiebacks with your curtains before cutting, for you can make your tiebacks a custom size very easily (just remember to adjust the fabric and interfacing requirements accordingly). To measure for a custom size, use your tape measure to make a trial tieback at your window, draping the curtains as desired. Note the tieback length needed. The width can be as narrow as your tape measure, or very wide, whatever looks best in proportion to your window treatment.

2. *Cut two matching fabric strips the finished tieback length plus 1" (2.5cm) for seams, and*

The Prime Place for Tiebacks

Where should you position tiebacks? Wherever you think they look the best. This takes a little experimenting, and it helps to have another person hold the tiebacks in place at the window for you. Then you can step back and see what kind of scoop they create along the pulled-back curtain edges.

Tiebacks tend to look best when not centered. Professional decorators often place tiebacks at three-fifths of the total length of the curtains, or in line with the window sill. Sometimes they position tiebacks low to make the window look taller—a clever way to create a pleasing optical illusion.

twice the finished width plus 1"
(2.5cm) for seams—for standard
size tiebacks, cut the strips 9" ×
19" (23 × 48cm). Cut the strips
crosswise so any fabric motifs,
textures, or color shadings match
the curtain panels.

3. Fold each strip in half along
its length with wrong sides together; press; open out each strip.
Fuse interfacing to the wrong
side of each strip, lining up the
interfacing with the crease on
each strip (A).

4. Right sides together, fold each
strip in half along its length.
Stitch the raw edges together in a

½" (13mm) seam, leaving an
opening for turning (B).

Trim across the corners, and
turn to the right side. Slipstitch
the opening closed (see HAND
STITCHES). Press.

5. Mark the center of each short
edge. Sew a ring ½" (13mm)
from the mark on the inside front
of each tieback, and at the mark
on the back edge (C).

6. Install cup hooks on the window frame or wall, fold the
tiebacks around the curtain, and
slip the rings onto the hooks to
hang the tiebacks.

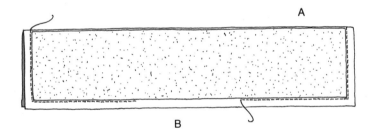

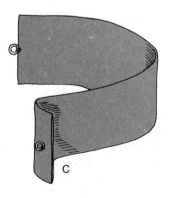

Sash Curtain Sash curtains differ from basic rod-pocket curtains in only one way. Instead of a bottom hem, there's a rod-pocket casing which matches the upper casing heading. Two sash or tension rods are needed to hang each sash curtain tier.

HOW-TO
Follow steps 1 to 6 for basic rod-pocket curtains (see page 91). Add an allowance for two casings to the finished length for each tier, and make a rod-pocket casing instead of a bottom hem (A).

A

Balloon Curtain The pouffed tiers of this curtain resemble a balloon shade and, like shades, the curtain can be raised and lowered. Use a sash rod or a tension rod to hang the curtain at the top of the window frame. In addition to fabric, you'll need a ½" (13mm) wooden dowel as long as the raw width of the curtain and 2 cup hooks to make the system which raises and lowers the curtain.

HOW-TO

1. *Measure and estimate fabric as if you were making sill-length rod-pocket curtains. (See pages 90–92). After determining the finished length, increase your fabric estimate by two-thirds to allow fabric for the top section of this curtain which folds down over the front to form the soft pouf at the top. Add a total of 4" (10cm) for the top and bottom casing. Also add 2" (5cm) extra fabric for loops.*

2. *Test the fabric for shrinkage and straighten the grain (see* CUTTING FABRIC*).*

3. *If more than one fabric width is needed for the panel, remember to match any designs at the seams; if working with fabric with a one-way sheen, texture, or design, use a with-nap cutting plan (see* CUTTING LAYOUTS*).*

4. *Trim off the selvages. If fabric widths must be seamed together, use French seams (see* SEAMS*).*

5. *Cut a 2" × 12" (5 × 31cm) crosswise strip for loops. On the remaining fabric, use a yardstick (meterstick) as a straight edge to mark the following lines straight*

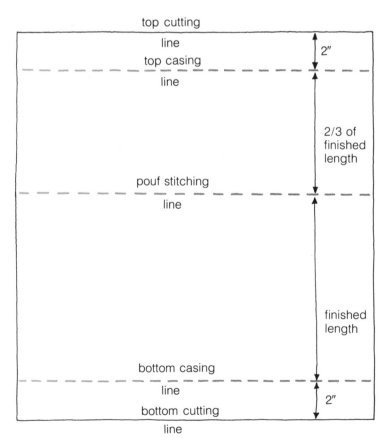

top cutting
line

2"

top casing
line

2/3 of
finished
length

pouf stitching
line

finished
length

bottom casing
line

2"

bottom cutting
line

across the wrong side of the curtain fabric: a bottom cutting line, a bottom casing line, a pouf stitching line, the top casing line, and the top cutting line. Space the lines apart the distances shown on the illustration. Cut out the panel on the cutting lines. If working with a plaid, stripe, or print, be sure to center any dominant motifs.

6. Stitch a 1" (2.5cm) double hem on each side of the curtain panel (see HEMS).

7. Fold under the bottom raw edge ½" (13mm); press. Fold up on the bottom casing line and stitch (A).

8. Use the crosswise strip to make two loops. (See TIES, DRAWSTRINGS AND LOOPS).

9. Fold under the top raw edge of the curtain panel ½" (13mm); press. Baste a loop 2" (5cm) in from each side, having all raw edges even (B).

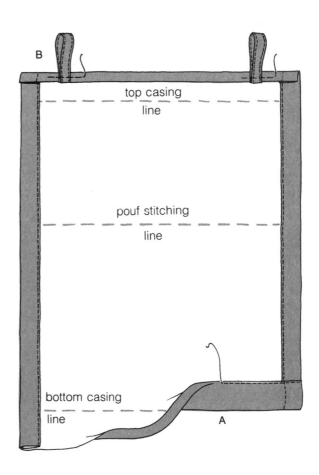

10. *With wrong sides together, bring the top casing line to the pouf stitching line. Pin in place, and stitch along the turned-under edge with the loops (C). Stitch again along the pouf stitching line (D).*

11. *Fold the curtain to the outside along the pouf stitching line and press. If desired, another row of stitching may be added by stitching through all layers from the wrong side along the previous stitching.*

12. *Insert the dowel in the bottom casing, arranging the curtain into even folds. Screw a cup hook through the casing into the dowel 2" (5cm) from the end (E). Insert the cup hooks so the hook end faces the window when the curtain is closed.*

13. *Insert the rod in the top casing, arranging the curtain into even folds. To raise the curtain, hook the cup hooks into the loops at the top of the curtain.*

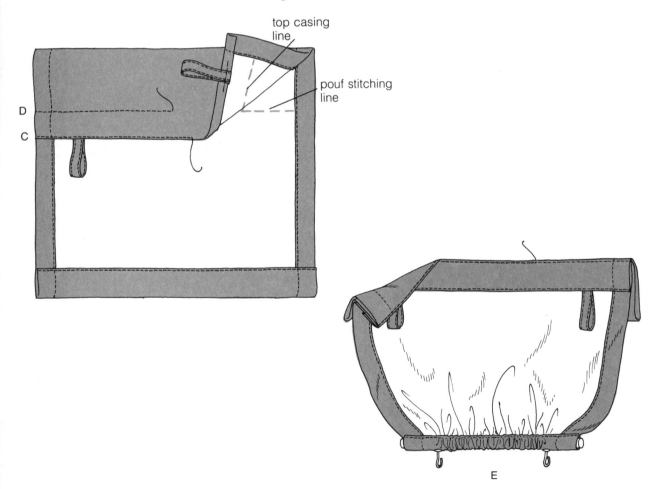

ROD-POCKET CURTAINS
WITH RUFFLES

Ruffled curtains are perennial favorites because they create such a wonderful atmosphere in a room. Ruffles look cozy and informal when made from a mini-print, soft and frilly when made from a floral sheer or embroidered eyelet, and simply elegant when cut from a formal fabric such as moiré or damask. As you measure to determine the finished length and width of the window treatment, remember that ruffles on the bottom of the curtain will increase the length, and ruffles on the sides will increase the width.

Most of the time, ruffled curtains are finished with tiebacks. Make basic tiebacks (see page 95), or use the tieback variations included with the projects in this section.

Center Ruffles The panels of this rod-pocket curtain have ruffles on the inner side edges only. Narrow ties are used as tiebacks, so in addition to fabric, you'll need 2 cup hooks and 2 small plastic rings.

HOW-TO

1. *Measure the curtain rod and estimate fabric requirements (see pages 85–89). Allow a ⅝" (15mm) seam allowance for the side of each panel which will be trimmed with a ruffle and a 1" (2.5cm) double hem for the opposite side hem. Measure around the rod to decide how much to allow for the rod-pocket casing, then add 4" (10cm) for the self-ruffle heading, and ¼" (6mm) for turning under the raw edge. Al-*

low for a 3" (7.5cm) double bottom hem.

The ruffles shown are cut 3¼" (8.2cm) wide for a finished width of 2" (5cm); estimate the fabric required for the ruffles and add it to the basic fabric estimate (see RUF-FLES). Add extra fabric for the two tiebacks, each 2" (5cm.) × the length desired.

2. *Test the fabric for shrinkage and straighten the grain (see CUT-TING FABRIC).*

3. *Follow step 3 for basic rod-pocket curtains to cut the fabric for the curtains (see page 91). Also cut the two strips for the tiebacks, and enough 3¼" (8.2cm) wide strips to make a ruffle for each curtain panel.*

4. *Trim off the selvages. If it's necessary to piece fabric widths for each curtain panel, or to piece the ruffle strips, use French seams (see* SEAMS*).*

5. *Hem the outer side edge and the bottom edge of each panel (A). Narrow hem one long edge and one short edge of each ruffle strip. Be sure to hem the inside edge of both ruffles (B).*

6. *Make a plain ruffle and gather it to fit the remaining side of each panel, reducing the amount of gathering in the casing area. Right sides together, stitch the ruffles to the panel sides in a ⅝" (15mm) seam and finish the seams (see* RUFFLES *for gathering and finishing techniques; C). Press the finished seam toward the panel so the ruffle extends out from the side edge.*

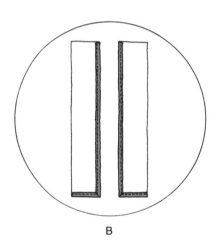

B

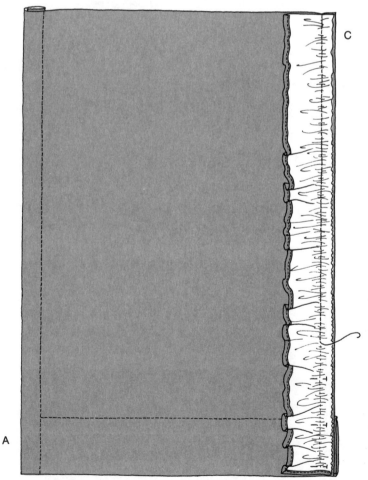

C

A

7. *For the rod-pocket heading, make a casing with a self-ruffle (see* CASINGS*) (D).*

8. *Use the 2" (5cm) wide strips to make two ties for tiebacks (see* TIES, DRAWSTRINGS, AND LOOPS*).*

9. *Hang the curtains on the rod and arrange them into even folds. Arrange a tieback around one panel and make a bow with the ends to mark the position for the ring. Sew a ring in place on the back of each tieback (E). Install cup hooks on the wall or window frame for the tieback rings (F).*

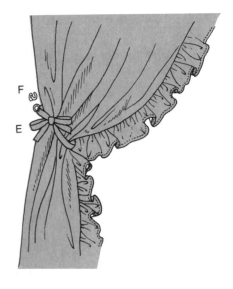

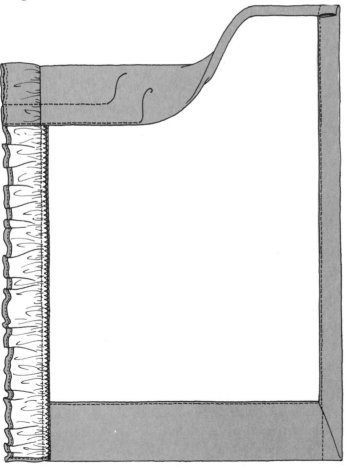

D

Ruffles with a Valance Feminine curtains like these look
best in an airy, sheer fabric,
preferably an easy-care type
which doesn't require ironing.
In addition to fabric, you'll need
4 small plastic rings and 2 cup
hooks to make the matching
tiebacks. Make a rod-pocket valance (see page 113), and hang
both curtains and valance on a
double curtain rod.

HOW-TO

1. Measure the curtain rod and estimate fabric requirements (see pages 85–89), adding a ⅝" (15mm) hem allowance for each side and bottom edge.

Measure around the rod to decide how much to allow for the rod-pocket casing.

The ruffles shown are cut 5¾" (14.5cm) wide for a finished width of about 4½" (11.5cm); estimate the fabric required for the ruffles and add it to the fabric estimate (see RUFFLES).

Add enough extra fabric for the matching tiebacks. You'll need two strips 5¾" (14.5cm) × the desired length for the tiebacks, and two strips 5¾" (14.5cm) × twice the desired length for the tieback ruffles.

2. Test the fabric for shrinkage and straighten the grain (see CUTTING FABRIC).

3. Follow step 3 for basic rod-pocket curtains to cut the curtain panels (see page 91). Also cut enough strips for the curtain ruffles, two strips for the tiebacks, and two strips for the tieback ruffles.

4. Trim off the selvages. If it's necessary to piece fabric widths for the curtain panels or the ruffle strips, use French seams (see SEAMS).

Make a template and round off the lower inner corner of each curtain panel (see TEMPLATES).

5. Narrow hem the sides and bottom of each panel, and all the edges of each ruffle (see HEMS).

6. Gather each ruffle near one long edge using two rows of long machine stitches or special quick-gathering techniques (see GATHERS ON A LARGE SCALE). Pin the wrong side of the ruffle to the right side of the inner edge and the bottom edge on each curtain panel. Make sure you pin and check both panels before stitching. You should have a right and a left curtain panel. Position the top of the ruffle just beneath the casing (A). Stitch the ruffle to the panel (B), and remove the gathering stitches.

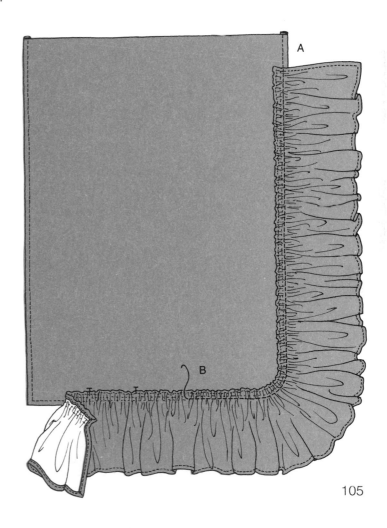

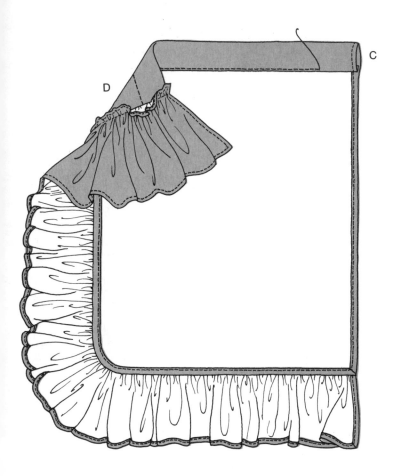

7. *Turn under the raw edge at the top of the curtain ¼" (6mm); press. Fold the casing into sewing position (C). Stitch the casing, keeping the edges of the ruffle free (D).*

8. *Fold each tieback section in half along its length, with right sides together. Stitch the raw edges together in a ⅝" (15mm) seam, leaving an opening for turning.*

Trim the seam; turn to the right side. Press. Slipstitch the opening closed (see HAND STITCHES*).*

Narrow hem, gather, and stitch a ruffle to the long seamed edge of each tieback (E), using the same techniques as for the curtain ruffle.

Slip each end of each tieback through a ring. Fold over the ends of the tieback and slipstitch in place (F).

9. *Hang the curtains on the rod and arrange them into even folds. Install a cup hook on the wall or window frame for the tieback rings.*

TAB-TOP CURTAINS

Tab-top curtains have open headings with loops, ties, or rings to show off decorative curtain rods beautifully. Tab-top curtains can be made in several tiers as café curtains, or as a pair of panels for a window. With the exception of the heading, tab-top curtains are made like basic rod-pocket curtains.

Tab-top with Loops and Scallops A crisp fabric such as sailcloth or chintz works well for this curtain style. If your fabric is too soft, the heading will droop instead of holding its shape. For a faster version of this curtain, just omit the scallops and sew the heading straight across. In addition to fabric, you'll need a lightweight, fusible interfacing to add body to the heading.

HOW-TO

1. *Measure your curtain rod and estimate the fabric requirements (see pages 85–89). Use the standard 1" (2.5cm) side and 3" (7.5cm) doubled bottom hem allowances, but add just 5/8" (15mm) for a seam allowance on the top.*

To determine how much extra fabric to allow for the loops and facing on the curtain heading, draw a full-sized pattern for the scalloped edge the finished width of the curtain. Use a round template (see TEMPLATES) and notch it to make a scallop; the scallop shown is 4½" (11.5cm) deep, but you can make a slightly different size scallop if desired. To space the scallops evenly on your pat-

tern, begin by drawing the first scallop ¾" (20mm) from one side edge (A). Space the remaining scallops ¾" (20mm) apart across the pattern, leaving ¾" (20mm) between the last scallop and the side edge (B); it may be necessary to increase or decrease the fin-

ished width of the curtain panel slightly to do this. Add a ⅝" (15mm) seam allowance across the scallop edge.

Allow enough extra fabric to cut a facing 2" (5cm) deeper than the scallops × the finished width of the curtain panel plus 1" (2.5cm). Buy enough fusible interfacing to back the facing. Allow enough extra fabric to cut one loop for each scallop point and each side edge—each loop is 3" (7.5cm) × the length needed to encircle the rod easily plus 1¼" (3.2cm) for seam allowances.

2. Test the fabric for shrinkage and straighten the grain (see CUTTING FABRIC).

3. Follow step 3 for basic rod-pocket curtains to cut the fabric

panels (see page 91). Also cut a facing for each panel, and a strip long enough to make all the loops.

Cut a strip of fusible interfacing 1" (2.5cm) shorter and narrower than each facing.

4. Trim off the selvages. If it's necessary to piece fabric widths together for the panels, use French seams (see SEAMS). Use plain seams to piece the facing sections.

5. On each panel, stitch the side hems first, then the bottom hem (see HEMS).

6. Position the interfacing ½" (13mm) from all edges of the facing, on the wrong side. Fuse, following the interfacing manufacturer's directions. Turn under one long facing edge ¼"

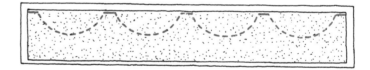

(6mm); press. Turn under both short edges ½" (13mm). On the opposite long edge use your paper pattern to mark the facing on the wrong side with the stitching lines for the scallops.

7. Make the required number of loops (see TIES, DRAWSTRINGS, AND LOOPS). Fold each loop in half, and pin the raw edges together.

8. Pin each facing to each curtain panel, right sides together. Slip a loop between the facing and curtain at each side edge and between each scallop (C); pin the loops in place.

Stitch the facing to the panel, taking a ⅝" (15mm) seam and stitching on the scallop stitching lines. Trim the seam allowance to ¼" (6mm), and clip diagonally across corners. Clip the curved seams of the scallops at close intervals, being careful not to cut into the stitches.

9. Turn the facing to the right side; press. Stitch the lower edge of the facing to the curtain. Slip-stitch the open ends of the facing to the curtain by hand (see HAND STITCHES).

10. Insert the curtain rod through the loops to hang the panels.

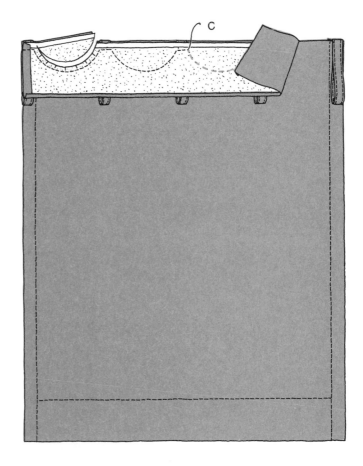

SHOWER CURTAINS

Almost any fabric used for window curtains can be used to make shower curtains, from embroidered eyelet to gingham to chintz, as long as you steer clear of delicate fabrics, which can be damaged by the moisture-laden air. If you use waterproof vinyl for your shower curtain, there's no need for a separate plastic liner.

Basic Shower Curtain This custom shower curtain has buttonholes at the top so the curtain and a purchased waterproof liner can hang on the same set of shower curtain hooks. If you've selected vinyl as your fabric, you'll need special sewing techniques (see FABRICS THAT REQUIRE SPECIAL HANDLING) and 12 large metal eyelets called grommets for the heading.

HOW-TO

1. *A standard-size shower curtain is 70" wide × 72" long (178 × 183cm), and requires about 4⅝ yds (4.25m) of fabric 44–45" or 54–55" (115 or 140cm) wide. If your fabric has a stripe, plaid, or print design which must be matched at the seams, add extra fabric equal to the length of three design repeats to this estimate.*

To make a shower curtain in another size, measure the length and width of the tub area to be covered by the curtain, add 4" (10cm) to the width and 1" (2.5cm) to the length measurement for seam/hem allowances,

and an extra ⅛ yd (0.15m) per panel for a 4½" (11.5cm) facing. Estimate fabric requirements using the formulas for curtains (see page 88). Since a shower curtain drapes flat when closed, you don't have to allow any extra fabric for fullness. Adjust the cut widths of the project sections given below to fit your tub area.

2. *Test the fabric for shrinkage and straighten the grain (see CUTTING FABRIC).*

3. *Cut a center panel 44" × 73" (112 × 185cm), and two side panels 15" × 73" (38 × 185cm). Also cut a facing 74" (188cm) wide × 4½" (11.5cm) deep for the top of the curtain. Cut this facing in three sections, like the curtain panels. If working with a plaid, stripe, or print, be sure to balance the motifs and match the design at the panel seams; if working with a fabric with a one-way surface sheen, texture, or design, use a with-nap cutting plan (see CUTTING LAYOUTS).*

4. *Use French seams (see SEAMS) to join the curtain panels. To piece the facing, use plain seams; press the seams open.*

5. *Finish the sides and bottom of the curtain with a narrow hem (A) (see HEMS).*

6. *Turn under the raw edge of the facing ⅝" (15mm) on the sides and bottom edge. Press. Right sides together, stitch the facing to the curtain along the*

top edge in a ⅝" (15mm) seam
(B). Trim the seam.

Turn the facing to the inside of
the curtain. Press. Stitch the
lower edge of the facing to the
curtain.

7. From the right side, stitch
close to the edge of the sides and
the bottom of the curtain, secur-
ing the free ends of the facing in
the stitching (C).

8. To mark the location for buttonholes in the curtain heading,
lay the purchased liner on top of
the shower curtain, lining up the
top edges, and mark through the
liner's heading openings. Make
machine buttonholes large
enough to accommodate the
shower curtain hooks at each
marking (D). Insert the hooks
through liner and curtain to hang
them on the rod.

To finish the heading on a
vinyl curtain, instead of buttonholes, hammer a grommet ¾"
(20mm) from each end. Space ten
more grommets equally in between.

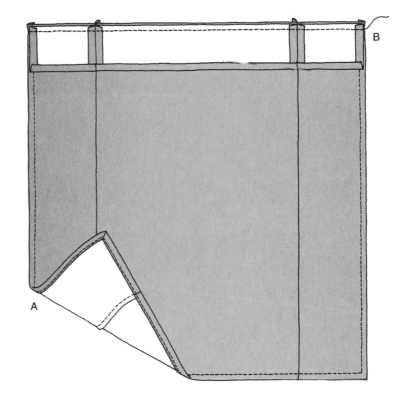

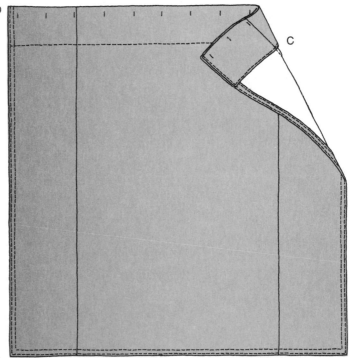

111

Valances and Swags

Valances and swags are used to top off window treatments. A valance looks like a short curtain, and a swag is a length of fabric draped over the top of the window in soft folds. If you're decorating on the light side, one of these window-top accessories can be the total window treatment, or you can add them to curtains, fabric shades, and nonfabric window treatments such as wooden shutters or metal blinds. Use valances and swags to carry out a decorating theme, to create the illusion of taller windows, or to hide hardware such as window shade brackets for a polished finish.

VALANCES

Use good judgment when deciding how long to make a valance—it should look balanced and in proportion to the entire window treatment. Most valances are 10″ to 15″ (25.5 to 38cm) long, or about one-sixth of the length of the window treatment. You may want to make a sample valance from paper or fabric to check the proportions. To take measurements, install the rod or other supporting hardware first, using a double rod to hang a valance over curtains. A separate projecting rod or a decorative pole rod can also be used for a valance.

An easy way to make a valance is to use the same sewing method that you used for the curtains—just make the valance

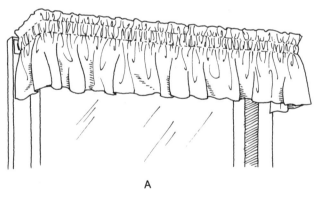

A

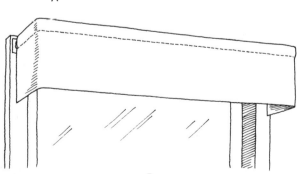

B

a shorter panel. Also adapt the sewing method to make the valance in one piece across the window, seaming together fabric widths as needed and making the bottom hem less deep. If you're making a flat or minimally full valance, it's a good idea to back the fabric with fusible interfacing before sewing hems and headings. This gives the valance enough extra body so it won't cup in toward the window.

The basic rod-pocket curtain method (see page 90) can be adapted easily to make a full valance (A), or a flat valance which needs no allowance for fabric fullness (B). Other curtain styles which seem like natural choices for valances are sash (see page 97) and tab-top curtains (see page 107). To make valances to match ruffled curtains (see page 101), add the ruffle to the bottom edge of the valance.

SWAGS

A swag which drapes across the window and cascades down the sides can be hung on a projecting rod, from the finials of a decorative pole rod, or from a pair of decorative metal holdbacks. Drawstrings attach the swag to the rod or holdbacks. Cut all in one piece and lined to the edge, a basic swag is very easy to make.

Basic Swag This method shows you how to trim a swag with ribbon and line it with self-fabric. If you prefer, you can substitute another band trim such as braid; insert a ruffle, lace, or fringe trim in the seam; or omit trims entirely. Another option is using a contrasting lining, an attractive way to emphasize the side cascades where the lining shows. Plus, the swag's reversible. With a contrasting lining, you can flip the swag over for a quick change in your decorating scheme.

Select a fabric that drapes gracefully. Crisp fabrics may be too stiff, and heavyweight fabrics too bulky, to drape into swags. Before you buy, unwind the fabric from the bolt and

stage a little test-draping in the store to see if you like the way the fabric reacts. If you're using self-fabric for a lining, do this with a double layer of fabric for a realistic appraisal of how the finished swag is going to look. In addition to fabric, you'll need 7/8″ (22mm) wide ribbon and, for the drawstrings, 4 to 6 yds (3.70 to 5.50m) of 1/8″ (6mm) cable cord.

HOW-TO

1. *Install the rod or holdbacks for the swag to take measurements. Measure the finished width across the window, between the rod brackets or the holdbacks (A). Measure the finished length from the top of the rod or the holdbacks to where you want the swag to end (B)—usually this is at the window sill or in line with the apron beneath the sill.*

2. *To estimate the fabric requirements, add the finished width and twice the finished length together. Divide by 36 (100) to convert this number into yards (meters). This gives you enough fabric to cut the swag; buy the same amount for the lining. The wider the fabric, the more folds and fabric fullness you'll have for draping at the center of the swag.*

To estimate how much ribbon trim you'll need, add the finished width, twice the finished length, and twice the fabric width together. Divide by 36 (100) to convert this number into yards (meters).

3. *Test the fabric for shrinkage and straighten the grain (see CUT-TING FABRIC). Preshrink the ribbon and cord.*

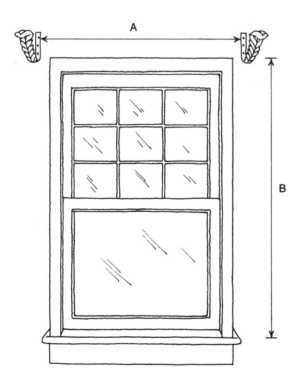

4. *Trim off the selvages. On the right side, mark the fabric at the center of one long edge (C). This mark will fall at the center of the window. Mark half the finished width of the swag on each side of the center (D). This is the top edge of the swag.*

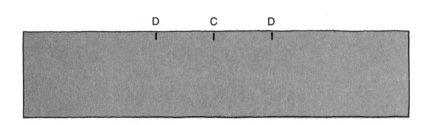

Tie a string around the swag at each of the finished width marks. Center the panel at the window, tying the strings around the ends of the rod or holdbacks to support the swag (E). Gently release the tied fabric to pull the swag down at the center to the depth desired (F). Make sure both side edges of the swag are even. Mark the points where the string now falls on the lower edge of the swag—these are where the casings will end (G). Also mark the points where you want the side cascades to begin (H). Remove the swag from the window and untie the strings.

To cut the sides of the swag, draw a line to connect the marks for the beginning of the side cascades with the ends of the top edge of the swag (I). Cut on these two lines and discard the triangles.

Mark the casing stitching lines on the right side of the fabric by connecting the finished width marks on the top edge to the casing end marks on the bottom edge of the swag (J).

Cut out a lining section to match.

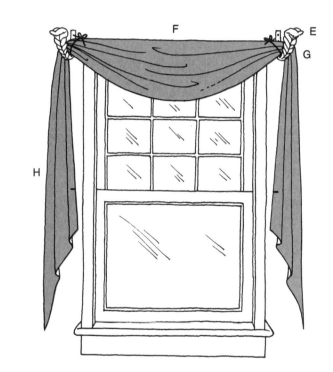

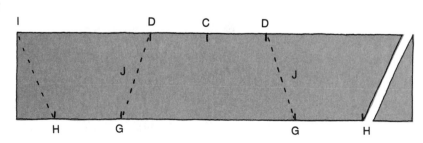

5. *To apply the ribbon, pin it to the right side of the swag about 2" (5cm) in from the bottom and side edges. Stitch close to both long edges of the ribbon.*

6. *Pin the swag to the lining with right sides together. Stitch around the edges in a ½" (13mm) seam, leaving a ¾" (20mm) opening at each end of the casing stitching lines (K) and an opening for turning along the top edge (L).*

Trim across the corners, and turn to the right side. Press.

Slipstitch the opening used for turning.

7. *Stitch along the casing stitching lines. Stitch again ⅜" (10mm) away on both sides of each casing stitching line to form two casings on each side of the swag (M).*

Cut the cord into 2 equal lengths. Insert a cord into each casing (N).

8. *Pull the cords to gather the swag. Tie the cords to the rod or holdbacks to hang the swag.*

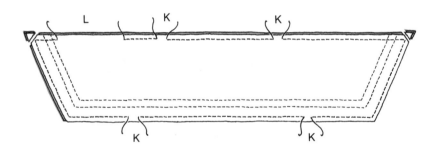

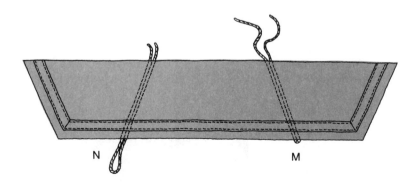

Shades

Versatile, practical, and virtually a symbol of custom decorating, fabric shades offer a fresh approach to dressing windows. There's a style of shade for every decorating scheme, from plain roller shades to tailored Roman, shirred Austrian, and pouffed balloon styles. Shades by themselves make a sophisticated window treatment, but you can also combine them with valances or tieback curtains if you like.

From a practical standpoint, shades can be raised to let in light and air, or lowered for privacy, and they're often just right for odd windows in problem places. Because shades cover only the window area, they won't invade precious wall and floor space—an important consideration if your rooms are small.

ROLLER SHADES

For shades which roll smoothly, choose a lightweight or mediumweight fabric. In addition to fabric, you'll need special shade hardware and supplies.

The easiest way to assemble the hardware for a fabric roller shade is to take apart an existing shade, or purchase an inexpensive shade for this purpose. Discard the shade body, but keep the wooden roller (A), the slat (B), and the brackets (C). Mount the brackets and take accurate measurements for the shade as described below.

Use fusible shade backing such as Style-A-Shade™ to make your fabric sturdy and crisp for the shade body. Shade backings come in 36″ and 45″ (91.5 and 114.5cm) widths; you

can use the backing crosswise if necessary to avoid splicing wide shades. You'll also need a clear-drying glue such as Fray Check™ to seal the cut edges of the shade, and a staple gun or

tacks to attach the shade to the roller.

A slip-on plastic shade pull (D) prevents soiling. Decorative shade pulls with tassels or covered rings are also available.

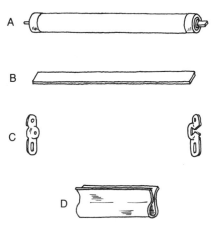

Basic Roller Shade This basic shade has a simple casing at the hem. A wooden slat fits into the casing.

HOW-TO

1. *Measure the window to determine the size of roller and slat to purchase. Use a steel measuring tape or a folding ruler for accuracy. Measure each window individually if you're sewing shades for several windows, for the windows may not be identical.*

The brackets for roller shades are usually installed inside the window frame. This hides the supporting hardware for a neat finish, but requires careful fitting with little margin for error. If you prefer, you can mount shades on the frame itself. Measure across the window between the points where you plan to install the brackets.

2. *Mount the brackets on the window frame. Make sure the brackets are installed on the level so the finished shade will hang square and roll smoothly.*

Notice the brackets are of two different types. One bracket has a hole in it—the round pin at the end of the window shade roller fits into this bracket (A). The other bracket has a slot opening—the flat pin at the end of the roller fits into this bracket (B). For a shade with a conventional roll—the shade rolls toward you as it's raised—mount the bracket for the flat pin on the left-hand side of the window, and the bracket for the round pin on the right (C). For a shade with a reverse roll—the shade rolls toward

the window—mount the brackets vice versa (D).

3. *To take the measurements for the shade, insert the roller in the brackets. Measure the width of the shade across the top of the roller, between the brackets, and subtract ⅛" (3mm) for shade clearance. This is the finished width of the shade.*

Measure the length from the top of the roller to the window sill, and add 12" to 16" (30.5 to 40.5cm) to allow extra fabric to remain on the roller when the shade is fully drawn. This is a necessary safety margin to maintain the spring tension in the

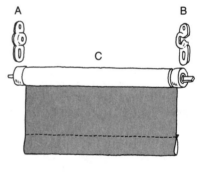

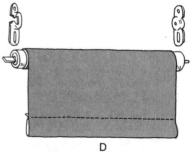

roller. Also add a 1½" (3.8cm) hem allowance. This is the total length of the shade.

4. To avoid splices, which spoil the appearance of the shade, buy fabric at least as wide as the finished width of the shade, plus 1" to 2" (2.5 to 5cm) to allow for trimming the edges. Buy enough fabric to equal the total shade length, plus 1" to 2" (2.5 to 5cm) trimming allowance.

Buy the same amount of fusible shade backing.

5. Test the fabric for shrinkage and straighten the grain (see CUT-TING FABRIC).

6. Cut the fusible shade backing to the same size as the shade fabric.

7. To fuse the fabric and backing, first press the fabric so it's free from wrinkles. Place the fabric right side down, then position the backing fusible side down on the fabric. Make sure no raveled threads or lint come between the fabric and backing; these will show through the finished shade.

Fuse, following the backing manufacturer's directions for the heat setting on your iron, and for the length of time and amount of pressure required. Work from the center toward the edges. Let the shade cool completely.

For a sound bond on some fabrics, it may be necessary to repeat the fusing, working from the fabric side. Use a press cloth for this to protect your fabric.

8. Mark the fabric with cutting lines according to the shade length and width including the trimming allowance. Center any prominent print motifs, stripes, or plaids, and plan to have a whole motif fall at the finished hem edge, about 1½" (3.8cm) from the raw edge at the bottom of the shade.

Use a ruler to draw the shade cutting lines for the finished width and total length. Draw on the backing lightly with a pencil. Use sharp shears to cut the shade to size.

To seal the raw edges and prevent raveling, paint glue or Fray Check™ very lightly on the edges with your fingertip. Allow the glue to dry thoroughly.

9. Turn 1½" (3.8cm) to the wrong side for the bottom casing.

Stitch close to the cut edge (E), or use a narrow strip of fusible web to bond the raw edge to the backing.

10. Remove the roller from the brackets. Position the top edge of the shade straight across the roller, with the flat pin on your left for a conventional roll (F), or on your right for a reverse roll. Use masking tape to hold the shade in position. Use tacks or a staple gun to secure the shade to the roller.

11. Turn the flat pin to wind the spring, and insert the roller into the brackets. Slip the slat into the casing.

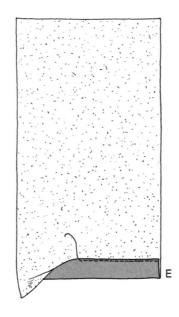

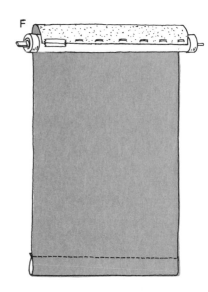

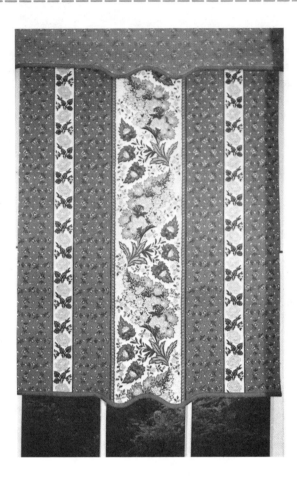

Shade with Shaped Hem This variation of the basic roller shade has a scalloped hem, one of the many ways you can shape the bottom of a shade to make it decorative. If you like, after you've made the shade, use the same design to shape the hem on a matching flat rod-pocket valance (see page 113). Use 1" (2.5cm) double-fold bias binding to trim the shaped hem.

HOW-TO

1. *Follow steps 1 through 7 for the basic roller shade above, adding an extra 4½" (11.5cm) to the length for the shaped hem. Buy enough bias binding to equal about 1½ times the finished shade width.*

2. *Use a ruler to draw on the backing with a pencil the shade cutting lines for the finished width and total length. To draw*

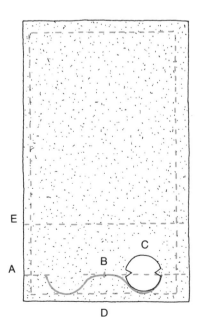

the cutting line for the shaped hem, begin with a straight line 1½" (3.8cm) above the bottom edge (A). Mark the center of the shade on this line (B). Notch a round template to draw two scallops (see TEMPLATES) about 2" (5cm) apart in the center, below the line (C). Make sure the scallops are symmetrical. Connect them with a slightly upward curved line (D).

Also mark a foldline for the slat casing 5½" (14cm) above the bottom edge (E).

Use sharp shears to cut the shade to size on the cutting lines as marked. Seal the cut edges by painting them lightly with glue or Fray Check™; let the glue dry.

3. Encase the shaped edge of the shade in bias binding (see BIAS TAPES AND BINDINGS).

4. With right sides together, fold the shade on the foldline which you marked for the casing (F). Press. Stitch 1½" (3.8cm) from the fold to form a casing (G) for the slat. Press the casing downward. Stitch close to the folded edge of the casing through all thicknesses (H).

5. Finish the shade by following steps 10 and 11 for the basic roller shade.

The Finishing Touch for Roller Shades

Keep fingers and soil off a shade by adding a shade pull. Slip-on plastic pulls are easy to install on any shade with a plain hem. To install cord pulls, punch a small hole through the center of the slat in the casing. Thread the pull through the hole. For a custom accent, you could also use a tassel on a cord as a shade pull.

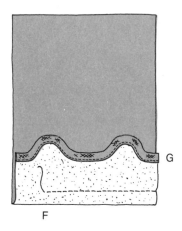

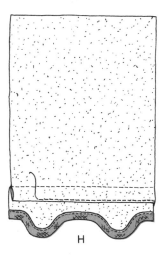

ROMAN SHADES

As the name implies, Roman shades have a handsome, classical look. When raised, these shades fold into a stack of pleats. If you use a lightweight fabric, the pleats are soft and gracefully bowed. Fabrics with a crisp finish, firm weave, or heavier weight fold into sharper, straighter pleats. In addition to fabric, you'll need special hardware and supplies.

On the shade body, use Roman shade tape, also called ring tape (A). To weight the bottom of the shade, you'll need a ½" (13cm) wooden dowel (B), or a round sash rod like those used for curtains. Lightweight tra-verse cord (C), nylon braided cord with a strong fiberglass core, is threaded through the rings to raise and lower the shade; you'll find traverse cord in stores which sell traverse rods for draperies, or use ⅛" (3mm) cable cord. A metal awning cleat (D) takes up the cord slack when the shade is raised.

Mounting the shade at the window requires a 1" × 2" (2.5cm × 5cm) wooden board (E), screw eyes (F), and angle irons (G). Attach the shade to the board with heavy-stress hook and loop tape such as Velcro® (H), and the tape to the board with tacks or staples.

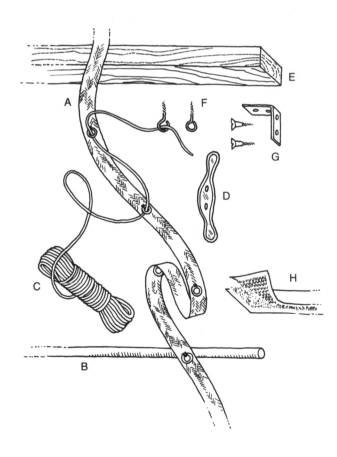

Basic Roman Shade This un-adorned Roman shade might be the perfect treatment for your windows, but there are many easy ways to add extras if you like. Make a shaped hem, for example (see page 120), or cover the tape stitching lines on the right side with ribbon, braid, or another band trim. Another creative option is making custom pleats. For this, sew extra plastic rings in between the presewn rings on the shade tape. You'll have twice as many pleats, half as deep, for a finer look when the shade is raised.

HOW-TO

1. The mounting board for a Roman shade is usually installed within the window frame, so measure across the window frame on the inside to determine the length of the board.

If you prefer, you can mount the board on the window frame or on the wall above the frame. Measure the length of the mounting board at the desired location.

To measure for the shade, install the angle irons which support the mounting board. Place the mounting board in position, but don't install it permanently at this time.

Measure the finished length *of the shade from the front of the mounting board to the window sill (A). The* finished shade width *is the length of the mounting board.*

2. For the total shade width, add 1¼" (3.2cm) to the finished width to allow for hemming the side edges. For the total shade length, add 2⅝" (6.7cm) to the finished shade length to allow for the hem and heading.

3. To estimate fabric requirements, divide the total shade width by the fabric width (minus the selvages, and minus 1" [2.5cm] for seam allowances)—this tells you the number of fabric widths needed. Round this off to the next highest whole number if necessary. Multiply the number of fabric widths times the total shade length to determine the amount of fabric needed; add enough extra fabric to cut a casing 2" (5cm) × the total shade width. Divide by 36 (100) to convert this number into yards (meters).

If your fabric is a plaid, print, or stripe, allow an extra design repeat per fabric width required. Also allow extra if you wish to cover the mounting board with shade fabric.

To estimate how much Roman shade tape to buy, divide the finished shade width by how far apart you wish to space the lengths of tape—generally no further apart than 12" (30.5cm). Then add 1. This tells you how many lengths of tape you'll need. Round this off to the nearest whole number if it didn't come out evenly, then multiply by the finished shade length to determine how much tape to buy. Divide by 36 (100) to convert this number into yards (meters).

To estimate how much cord to buy, add 1½ times the finished shade length to the finished shade width. Multiply this by the number of lengths of shade tape needed; divide by 36 (100) to convert this number into yards (meters).

The dowel or rod used to weight the bottom of the shade should be ¼" (6mm) shorter than the shade's finished width. Buy enough hook and loop tape to cover the length of the mounting board. Buy a screw eye for each length of tape, plus one extra screw eye.

4. Test the fabric for shrinkage and straighten the grain (see CUTTING FABRIC*). Also preshrink the tape.*

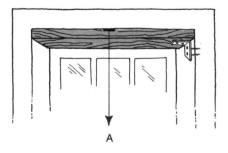

A

5. Work on a large, flat surface to mark and cut the fabric. Spread the fabric out smoothly, and trim off the selvages. Mark the cutting lines for the total length and total width of the shade. Center any prominent print, stripe, or plaid designs.

If more than one fabric width is needed, try to position the seams so they will be covered with a length of shade tape. Use ½" (13mm) plain seams, and press them open; trim the seam allowances to ¼" (6mm) so the Roman shade tape will cover the raw edges. Match prints, stripes, or plaids at the seams; if your fabric has a one-way surface sheen, texture, or design, use a with-nap cutting plan (see CUTTING LAYOUTS).

Also mark and cut a casing 2" (5cm) × the total width of the shade.

6. Finish the sides and bottom of the shade with a narrow hem (A) (see HEMS). For the heading, press under the raw edge ½" (13mm), then press under 1½" (3.8cm); stitch close to the edge (B).

7. Narrow hem the short ends of the casing. Turn under the long edges of the casing ¼" (6mm); press. Position the casing on the wrong side of the shade, with the lower edge of the casing 2" (5cm) above the bottom hem (C). Stitch close to both long edges of the casing.

8. Pin a length of Roman shade tape next to one side edge, posi-tioning the bottom ring just above the casing (D). Position the top of the tape 4" (10cm) below the top edge of the shade. Turn under both raw ends of the tape (E). Using a zipper foot, stitch around all edges of the tape (F).

It's important to have all the rings line up evenly across the shade, so use a yardstick (meterstick) to mark the placement for the remaining rings and tapes across the shade. Use a glue stick to position the tapes, then stitch them to the shade as described above. Position one length of tape next to the remaining side edge.

9. Stitch the loop half of the hook and loop tape on the inside of the shade heading (G).

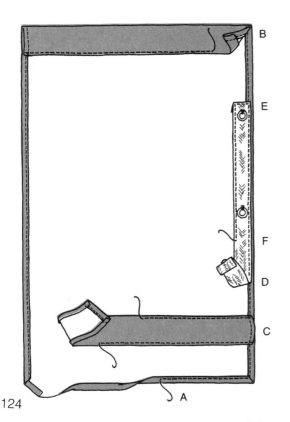

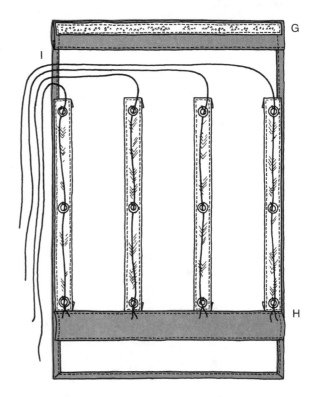

10. *Cut a length of cord for each length of tape; the length of each cord should equal 1½ times the finished shade length plus the shade width.*

Securely tie a cord to the bottom ring on each length of tape (H). Thread the cord up through the rings on the tape (I).

11. *If desired, paint the mounting board to match the window frame or the shade fabric, or cover the board with shade fabric using fusible web.*

12. *Staple or tack the hook half of the hook and loop tape across the front of the board (J).*

Press the hook and loop tape together to fasten the shade to the mounting board.

13. *Install a screw eye on the underside of the mounting board, behind each length of shade tape. Thread the cords through the screw eyes across the mounting board (K).*

Insert the dowel or rod in the shade casing. Adjust the tension in the cords so the shade hangs evenly and smoothly when fully lowered. Knot the cords together just beyond the last screw eye, then knot the ends together. Trim the cord ends evenly.

Install the awning cleat on the window frame about halfway down the shade and behind the side edge of the shade. Wrap the cords around the cleat to take up the cord slack when the shade is raised.

The Finishing Touch for Roman Shades

As soon as you install your Roman shade, raise it to its fully pleated position. Arrange the pleats in even folds, and leave them. After a few hours, raise and lower the shade several times, arranging the pleats each time until the fabric is "trained."

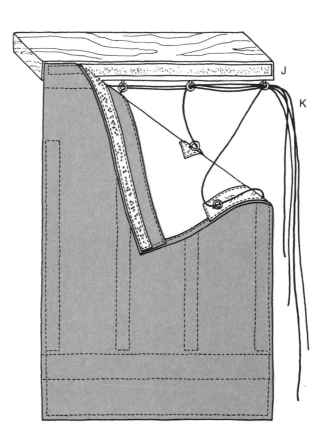

AUSTRIAN SHADES

Shirred to drape in elegant swags, Austrian shades have a formal, traditional look. A soft, lightweight fabric makes the best Austrian shades, and sheers such as lace and voile work especially well. In addition to fabric, you'll need special hardware and supplies.

On the shade body, use Austrian shade tape, which has rings and shirring cords (A), and across the top use 1" (2.5cm) wide 2-cord shirring tape (B) to gather the shade evenly. Weight the bottom of the shade with sew-on drapery weights (C). For the raise/lower system, use lightweight tra-

verse cord or ⅛" (6mm) cable cord (D), a metal awning cleat (E), a 1" × 2" (2.5 × 5cm) mounting board (F), screw eyes (G), and angle irons (H). To attach the shade to the mounting board, you'll also need heavy stress hook and loop tape and tacks or a staple gun to attach the tape to the board.

Basic Austrian Shade With its shirring, this basic shade is quite fancy as is. If you want to vary the styling to suit a period decor, use fringe to trim the bottom hem. You could go a step further and add a tassel at each swag point, too.

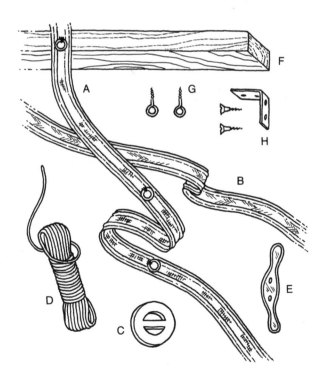

HOW-TO

1. *Follow step 1 for the Roman shade, above, to measure the mounting board, install the supporting angle irons, and measure the finished length and finished width of the shade.*

2. *For the* total shade width, *multiply the finished width by 1½, then add 1" (2.5cm) for turning under the raw edges.*

For the total shade length, *multiply the finished length by 3 for sheers, or 2 for other fabrics. Then add 4½" (11.5cm) to allow for the heading and the hem.*

Follow step 3 for the Roman shade to estimate fabric requirements (omit the casing allowance).

To estimate how much Austrian shade tape you'll need, decide how far apart you wish to space the lengths of tape—generally 12" (30.5cm) apart. Divide the total shade width by this number, then add 1. Round this off to the nearest whole number to determine the total number of tape lengths needed. Multiply the total number of tape lengths times the total shade length minus 2" (5cm) to determine how much tape to buy. Divide by 36 (100) to convert this number to yards (meters).

To estimate how much cord to buy, add 1½ times the finished shade length to the finished shade width; multiply this by the number of lengths of tape. Divide by 36 (100) to convert this number to yards (meters).

Buy a screw eye and a sew-on drapery weight for each length of tape.

Buy 2-cord shirring tape equal to two times the total width of the shade plus 2" (5cm).

3. *Test the fabric for shrinkage and straighten the grain (see* CUTTING FABRIC*). Preshrink the tapes.*

4. *Follow step 5 for the Roman shade to cut the shade fabric, omitting the casing.*

5. *Turn under ½" (13mm) on each side edge; press (A).*

Pin a length of Austrian shade

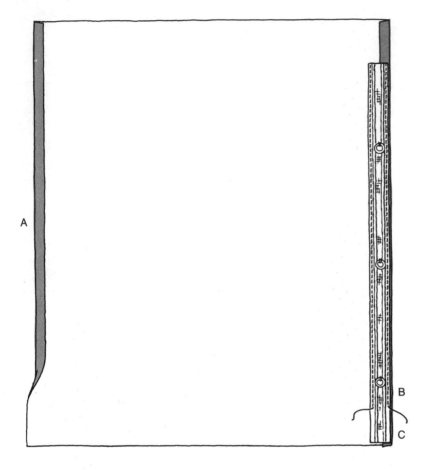

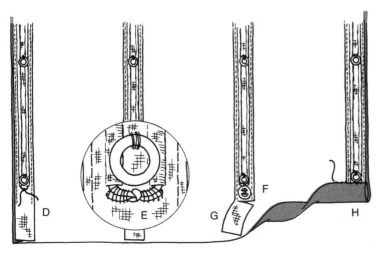

tape on one side edge, covering the raw edge. Place the bottom ring 3" (7.5cm) above the bottom edge (B), and end the tape 2¼" (5.7cm) from the top edge. Using a zipper foot, stitch close to both long edges of the tape, leaving the bottom 2" (5cm) of the tape unstitched (C).

It's important to have all the rings line up evenly across the shade, so use a yardstick (meterstick) to mark the placement for the remaining rings and tapes across the shade. Use a glue stick to position the tapes, then stitch them to the shade as described above. Position one length of tape next to the remaining side edge.

6. Use a pin to pick out the shirring cords on the tape below the rings at the bottom of the shade. Tie each set of cords in a secure knot (D). Whipstitch the cord ends to the tape (E) (see HAND STITCHES).

Sew a drapery weight to the tape below each bottom ring (F). Trim the tape below the weight (G).

7. To make the hem, turn up 1" (2.5cm), then fold up another 1" (2.5cm); press. Slipstitch the hem by hand (H).

8. At the top of the shade, pull the shirring cords on the shade tape to gather the shade evenly. Gather the shade until it measures the finished length plus 2½" (6.5cm). Tie each set of cords in a knot. Adjust the gathers so the rings are level across the shade.

9. *For the shade heading, fold under the raw edge ½" (13mm). Press. Cut the length of 2-cord shirring tape into two equal sec tions. Apply one section of shirring tape to the wrong side of the shade, covering the raw edge (I) (see* GATHERS ON A LARGE SCALE*). Apply the second section of tape next to the first, with the edges of the tape matching. Before stitching in place, cut off any rings on the Austrian shade tape that fall under the shirring tape.*

Pull the shirring cords to gather the shade evenly. Gather the shade until it measures the finished shade width. Tie the shirring cords securely.

10. *Follow steps 9–13 for the Roman shade to apply hook and loop tape, thread the cords, prepare the mounting boards, and*

mount the shade, omitting the reference to the dowel or rod at the shade hem.

11. *Use staples or tacks to fasten the shade heading to the top of the mounting board (J). Then install the shade at the window following step 13 for the Roman shade, omitting the dowel or rod at the shade hem.*

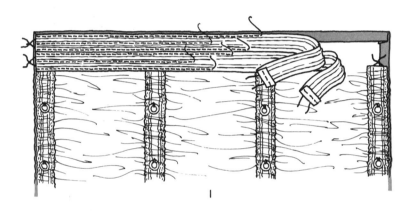

I

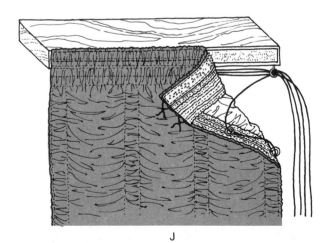

J

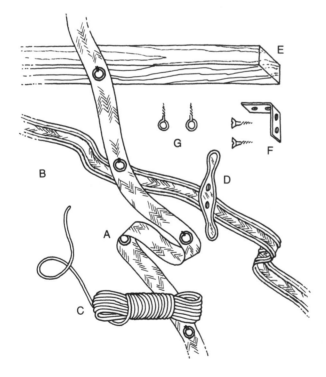

BALLOON SHADES

When raised, balloon shades form pouffed clouds of fabric, a soft yet dramatic look for beautiful windows. Lightweight fabrics such as broadcloth, gingham, dotted Swiss, and muslin make the best "balloons." Balloon shades are first cousins to Roman shades, and require many common supplies in addition to fabric.

On the shade body, use Roman shade tape with presewn rings (A), and across the top use 1" (2.5cm) wide 2-cord shirring tape (B) to gather the shade evenly. For the raise/lower system, buy lightweight traverse cord or ⅛" (6mm) cable cord (C), a metal awning cleat (D), a 1" × 2" (2.5 × 5cm) mounting board (E), angle irons (F), and screw eyes (G). To attach the shade to the mounting board, you'll also need heavy stress hook and loop tape and tacks or a staple gun to attach the tape to the board.

Basic Balloon Shade If you'd like to trim this shade, keep the trimming light and airy. Lace edging or a self-fabric ruffle could be added easily to the bottom edge, for example (be sure to include the ruffle allowance in your fabric estimate).

HOW-TO

1. *Follow step 1 for the Roman shade (see page 123) to measure the mounting board, install the supporting angle irons, and measure the finished length and finished width of the shade.*

2. *To determine the total length, add to the finished length at least 13" (33cm) for the hem, heading, and bottom fullness.*

To determine the total width, multiply the finished width by 2½, then add 1" (2.5cm) for turning under the raw edges.

Follow step 3 for the Roman shade to estimate fabric requirements, omitting the casing.

To estimate how much Roman shade tape you'll need, divide the total shade width by 12 to 15, because you'll need a length of tape about every 12" to 15" (30.5 to 38cm) for a nice billowing effect. Add 1, then round this off to the nearest whole number to determine the number of tape lengths needed. Multiply the number of tape lengths by the finished shade length to determine how much tape to buy. Divide by 36 (100) to convert this number to yards (meters).

To estimate how much cord to buy, add 1½ times the total shade length to the total shade width; multiply this by the number of lengths of tape needed. Divide by 36 (100) to convert this number to yards (meters).

Buy a screw eye for each length of tape.

Buy 2-cord shirring tape equal to two times the finished width of the shade plus 2" (5cm).

3. *Test the fabric for shrinkage and straighten the grain (see* CUT-TING FABRIC*). Preshrink the tapes.*

4. *To mark and cut the fabric, follow step 5 for the Roman shade, omitting the casing.*

5. *Turn under ½" (13mm) on the sides and top edge of the shade (A); press.*

Cut the length of shirring tape into two equal sections. Pin one

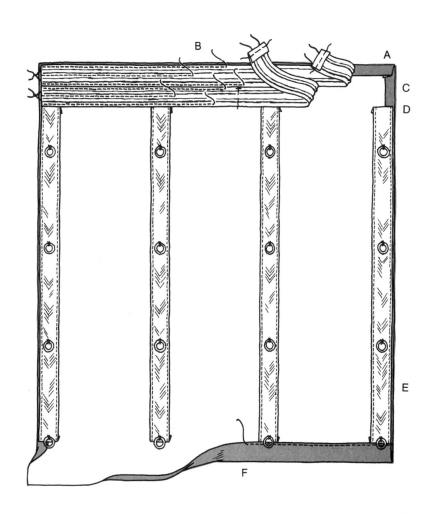

131

section of the shirring tape to the wrong side at the top of the panel, covering the raw edge (B). Stitch the tape in place (see GATHERS ON A LARGE SCALE). Apply the second section of tape next to the first with the edges of the tapes meeting.

6. Pin a length of Roman shade tape to one side edge, covering the raw edge (C). The bottom ring should be 2" (5cm) above the bottom edge of the shade. Turn under the raw edge of the tape 1/4" (6mm) at the top edge, just below the shirring tape (D). Turn under the raw edge at the bottom just under the bottom ring on the tape. Stitch both long edges of the Roman shade tape (E).

It's important to have all the rings line up evenly across the shade, so use a yardstick (meterstick) to mark the placement for the remaining rings and tapes across the shade. Use a glue stick to position the tapes, then stitch them to the shade as described above. Position one length

of tape next to the remaining side edge.

7. To make the hem, fold under the raw edge 1/4" (6mm), press, then turn up the edge 1" (2.5cm). Press. Topstitch (F) or blindstitch the hem by machine, keeping the rings free.

8. Pull the cords in the shirring tape heading to gather the shade evenly, to measure the finished width of the shade. Knot the cords to secure them.

9. Follow steps 9–13 for the Roman shade to apply hook and loop tape, thread the cords, prepare the mounting board, and mount the shade, omitting the reference to the dowel or rod at the shade hem.

10. Use staples or tacks to fasten the shade heading to the top of the mounting board. Then install the shade at the window following step 13 for the Roman shade, omitting the dowel or rod at the shade hem.

The Finishing Touch for Balloon Shades

To form the fabric into full, soft poufs, raise the shade and tuck tissue paper into the folds. Keep the tissue in place long enough to "train" the fabric into shape. As long as it doesn't show from the outside of the window, you could even leave the tissue in place—decorators often do this for picture-perfect balloon shades.

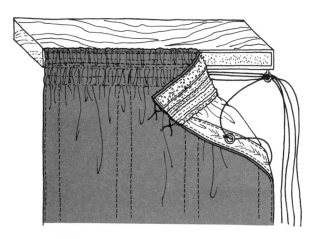

Bed Treatments

Because a bed takes up such a large area in a bedroom, the way you dress the bed automatically makes it the focal point. As a focal point, it can be tailored or full of frills—whatever you find inviting. For such a personal room, use fabric which creates a wonderful atmosphere, from filmy sheers to rugged corduroy, from cozy quilted broadcloths to sensuous silks and satins. The methods for making bed treatments are adaptable to many decorating styles and types of fabrics, so why not take this opportunity to create the bedroom of your dreams?

On the following pages, how-to's for these kinds of projects are given:

- Coverlets, from simple throws to fitted styles.

- Comforters filled with soft, fluffy batting for beds of all sizes, and quilts for cribs.

- Dust ruffles, in both pleated and gathered versions, to complete your bed treatment.

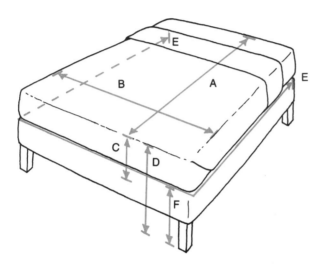

MEASURING BEDS

Make up the bed with the sheets and blankets normally used on the bed, then take the measurements with a tape measure or flexible steel tape.

Coverlets Coverlets cover the mattress area and are used in tandem with a dust ruffle which covers the boxspring. Since coverlets do not cover the pillows, you can finish the bed treatment with a set of matching bed pillow shams (see page 170).

For the coverlet's finished length, measure from the head to the foot of the bed (A). For the finished width, measure from side to side across the bed (B). For the drop, measure from the top of the mattress to about 2″ (5cm) below the top of the box spring (C) or to the floor (D).

Comforters Measure for the finished length, finished width, and drop as described for coverlets. Since comforters are filled with batting, add about 6″ (15cm) to the drop to allow for "shrinkage" when the filler puffs up the fabric layers.

Dust Ruffles Measure for the finished length along the top of the boxspring, beginning at one corner at the head of the bed. Continue around the edge of the boxspring to the other corner (E). Measure the drop (depth) from the top of the boxspring to the floor (F).

Making a Full-length Bedspread

To make a bedspread instead of a coverlet, just begin with a slightly different set of measurements. Measure the bed as described for coverlets, except measure the drop all the way to the floor. If you want your bedspread to cover the bed pillows, take the finished length measurement with the pillows in place, then add a tuck-in allowance of about 10″ to 15″ (25.5 to 38cm).

Coverlets

Coverlets can be made in several styles. Throws are the easiest to make, for they're just rectangles of fabric with two corners rounded off. Fitted coverlets, on the other hand, are made in several sections. On the top is a flat panel fitted to the top of the mattress. The drop at the sides is made in separate sections, and can be pleated for a tailored look, or gathered into a wide ruffle called a flounce.

THROW COVERLETS

Perhaps because they're styled so simply, throws are often trimmed. The basic style has welting at the edge, a handsome trim which also adds body and shape so the rounded corners flare nicely. Some of the other trims you could use are lace edging, a self-fabric ruffle, braid, and wide bias binding. Another easy variation is lining the throw to the edge—just make a lining to match the throw, and stitch them both together around the edge, leaving an opening for turning. If you use a contrasting fabric, your throw will be reversible.

Basic Throw Coverlet Select a striped or plaid fabric to cover the cord, and this throw will have diagonal lines along the welted edge, accenting this stylish detail. In addition to fabric, you'll need ¾" (20mm) piping cord to make the welting.

HOW-TO

1. Measure the bed (see page 134).

2. Determine the total width by adding twice the drop to the finished width, plus 1¼" (3.2cm) for finishing the edges. Determine the total length by adding the drop to the finished length, plus 1¼" (3.2cm) for finishing the edges.

To estimate fabric, divide the total width by the fabric width (minus selvages and 1¼" [3.2cm] for seam allowances). This tells you how many panels of fabric you'll need to piece together to make the coverlet. Round this off to the next highest whole number if it doesn't come out evenly. Most coverlets require two or three fabric widths.

Multiply the number of panels times the total length for the amount of fabric needed. If you're using a stripe, plaid, or large print, also add the length of one design repeat per panel for balancing the design and matching it at the seams. Divide by 36 (100) to convert this number into yards (meters).

Use the Estimating Bias Yield chart (see page 35) to estimate the fabric needed to cover the welting trim.

To estimate how much cord to buy, add twice the total length to the total width, and add a few extra inches (cm) for easing the cord around the corners and finishing the ends. Divide by 36 (100) to convert this number into yards (meters).

3. Test the fabric for shrinkage and straighten the grain (see CUTTING FABRIC).

4. Work on a large, flat surface to mark and cut the fabric. Use a yardstick (meterstick) as a straight edge for drawing the cutting lines. Mark the cutting lines for the total width and total length measurements. Don't include the selvages, which are tightly woven and can cause puckered seams. If you're working with a stripe, plaid, or large print motif, be sure to balance the design (see CUTTING FABRIC).

If you're piecing panels, plan to cut at least three—one full fabric-width panel for the center, and two equal, partial width panels for each side (see SEAMS). Allow ⅝" (15mm) for seams on each edge, and remember to match any plaids, stripes, or large print motifs at the seams. If your fabric has a one-way sheen, texture, or design, use a with-nap cutting plan.

5. Cut bias strips 3¾" (23cm) wide to cover the cord, and make the welting (see WELTING).

6. Piece the coverlet panels together using French seams or mock French seams (see SEAMS).

7. To round off the two corners at the foot of the coverlet, fold the coverlet in half along its length (A). Line up two corners evenly, and mark them in a square which has sides the length of the drop (B). Use a ruler to mark the drop from the inner corner of the

square to the corner diagonally opposite (C). Draw a curved cutting line from this mark to the other two corners of the square. Cut out both corners on the curved line. Unfold the coverlet.

8. Finish the head edge of the coverlet with a narrow hem (see HEMS).

9. Pin the welting to the right side of the remaining edges of the coverlet, extending the welting ends ½" (13mm) (D). Clip into the welting seam allowances at the coverlet corners if necessary to ease the welting around the curves.

Pull out the cord and cut off ½" (13mm) at each end (E). Pick out the stitches to turn under the raw edges of the bias fabric covering. Make sure the turned-under edges are even with the hemmed coverlet edge (F). Slipstitch the ends of the welting closed (see HAND STITCHES).

Use a zipper foot to stitch the welting to the coverlet in a ⅝" (15mm) seam (G).

10. Leaving the welting seam allowance on the bottom untrimmed, trim the coverlet and remaining welting seam allowance to barely ¼" (6mm) (H). Turn under ⅛" (3mm) on the untrimmed welting seam allowance and pin over the seam. Use a zipper foot to stitch close to the fold (I).

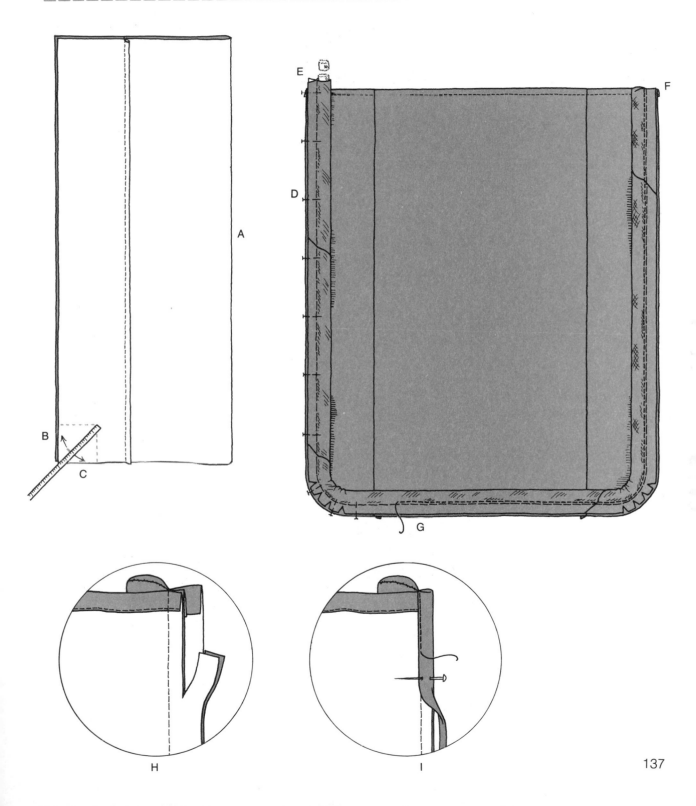

Throw Coverlet with Eyelet Edging In addition to fabric, you'll need eyelet edging to make this throw. Edging 1½″ (3.8cm) wide is used here, but you can use a wider edging if you prefer.

HOW-TO

1. *Measure the bed (see page 134).*

2. *Follow step 2 for the basic throw coverlet to estimate fabric requirements. Omit the cording and the extra fabric for welting.*

To estimate how much edging to buy, add the total width and twice the total length together. Add extra for finishing the ends—about 2" (5cm). Divide by 36 (100) to convert this number into yards (meters).

3. *Test the fabric for shrinkage and straighten the grain (see* CUT-TING FABRICS). *Preshrink the eyelet edging.*

4. *Follow steps 4, 6, and 7 for the basic throw coverlet above to cut and piece the fabric panels and round off the corners.*

5. *Trim straight across the uneven raw edge of the eyelet edging. Right sides together, pin the eyelet edging along the sides and foot of the coverlet (A); ease in extra edging around the curved corners and trim the raw ends of the edging even with the raw edge at the head of the coverlet. Stitch in a ⅝" (15mm) seam (B).*

6. *Finish the seam allowances (see* SEAMS). *Press the seam toward the coverlet.*

7. *Make a narrow hem across the head of the coverlet, including the raw edges of the eyelet edging as you sew (see* HEMS).

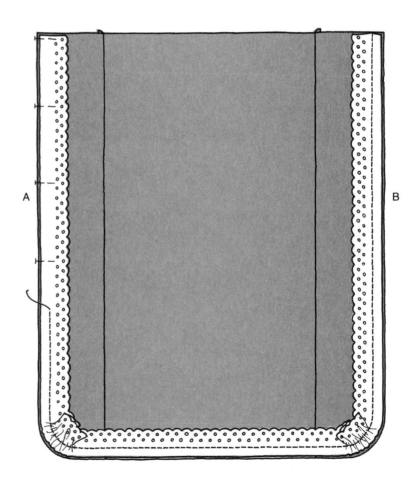

FITTED COVERLETS

Because fitted coverlets are made in two distinct sections—the top and the drop—they're prime candidates for creative fabric interplays. You could cut the top section from quilted fabric and the drop from matching unquilted fabric, for example. Or use twin prints for a subtle contrast between the two sections. For the flounced version, you could cut the top from plain batiste, and the drop from embroidered eyelet batiste, positioning the eyelet border so it forms a ready-made hem.

Fitted Coverlet with Flounce
This style of bed covering has a gathered drop which is called a flounce. The top of the coverlet is lined to the edge to provide an extra layer of fabric to support the weight of the flounce.

HOW-TO

1. *Measure the bed (see page 134).*

2. *Determine the total width for the top section by adding 1¼" (3.2cm) for seams to the finished width. Determine the total length for the top section by adding 1¼" (3.2cm) for seams to the finished length.*

To estimate how much fabric you'll need for the top section, divide the total width by the fabric width (minus selvages and 1¼" [3.2cm] for seam allowances). This tells you how many panels of fabric you'll need to piece together to make the top section. Round this off to the next highest whole number if it doesn't come out evenly. Most top sections require one, two, or three fabric-width panels, depending upon bed size and fabric width.

Multiply the number of panels times the total length to estimate the fabric required for the top section. If you're working with a stripe, plaid, or large print, add the length of one design repeat per panel so you'll have extra fabric for balancing the design and matching it at the seams.

Determine the total length of the drop by adding twice the finished length of the top section to the finished width of the top section. Double this to allow for fabric fullness, then add 3¾" (9.5cm) for finishing the edges. Determine the total depth of the drop by adding 1¼" (3.2cm) for seams and hems to the drop measurement. Estimate the fabric using the formulas given for ruf-

fles (see RUFFLES). Allow extra fabric if you're working with a stripe, plaid, or large print.

Add the fabric estimates for the top and drop sections together to determine the total fabric estimate. Use only the fabric estimate for the top to buy the lining fabric.

3. Test the fabric for shrinkage, and straighten the grain (see CUTTING FABRIC). Do the same for the lining.

4. Cut the fabric for the top section by following step 4 for the basic throw coverlet (see page 136). Cut the lining to match.

Cut the crosswise strips for the flounce. Remember to match stripes, plaids, and large prints at the seams.

5. If it's necessary to piece panels for the top section, use plain ⅝" (15mm) seams, and press them open. Do the same for the lining.

6. Make a template for the curved corners at the foot of the bed by slipping a piece of cardboard between the mattress and box spring (A). Trace the outline of the mattress onto the cardboard, and cut out the curve.

Use the template to round off

the two corners at the foot of the bed on the top section. Cut the lining to match.

7. With right sides together, pin the top section and the lining together. Stitch the edges together in a ⅝" (15mm) seam, leaving an opening for turning (B). Trim across the square corners diagonally (C), and notch the seam allowance of the curved corners (D). Trim the entire seam allowance.

Turn to the right side through the opening. Slipstitch the opening closed (see HAND STITCHES).

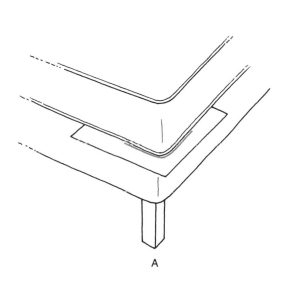

A

B   C

D

141

8. Join the flounce strips with French seams (see SEAMS) into three separate sections. Make one flounce section as long as twice the finished width of the coverlet top; this will form the flounce at the foot end of the coverlet. Make the other two sections as long as twice the finished length of the top section; these will form the flounces at the sides of the coverlet.

Finish all the raw edges of each flounce section with a narrow hem (see HEMS).

Gather the foot flounce ½" (13mm) from one long edge, using quick gathering techniques (see GATHERS ON A LARGE SCALE). With the **wrong side** of the flounce to the **right side** of the coverlet, lap the flounce ¾" (20mm) over the foot of the coverlet and bring it around the curved corners dis-

tributing gathers so that there is more fullness around the corners (E). Stitch the flounce to the coverlet ½" (13mm) from the flounce edge (F).

In the same way, gather and stitch the side flounces to the coverlet sides; lap the side flounces 1" (2.5cm) over the foot flounce at the curved corners (G). Remove the gathering stitches.

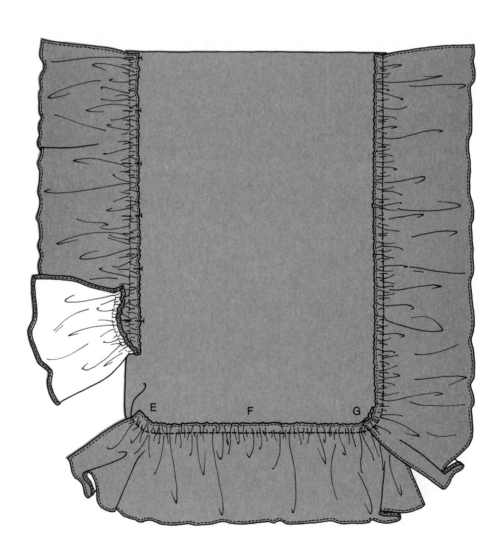

Fitted Coverlet with Pleats
Grosgrain ribbon is a perfect tailored trim for a fitted coverlet with a box pleat at each foot-of-the-bed corner. For this coverlet, ⅞" (22mm) wide ribbon trim was used, but you could use ribbon of another width if you prefer. For neat, crisp pleats, choose a medium-weight fabric that has plenty of body, such as raw silk, chintz, or sateen.

HOW-TO

1. *Measure the bed (see page 134).*

2. *Determine the total width, total length, and fabric required for the top section by following step 2 for the fitted coverlet with flounce, above, but use the following method to determine the fabric required for the drop panels.*

To determine the total width of the two side panels and the foot panel, add 1¾" (4.5cm) for seam and hem allowances to the drop. For the total length of each side panel, add 6" (15cm) for seam and pleat allowances to the finished length of the top section. For the total length of the foot panel, add 31" (79cm) for seam and pleat allowances to the finished width of the top section.

To avoid unnecessary seams, each of these three panels should be cut in one piece with the lengthwise grain running along the long edges. If your fabric is wide enough, you may be able to cut all three from one fabric width; in this case, the fabric required will be equal to the total length of one side panel or the foot panel, whichever is longer. If you can cut just two panels from one fabric width, the fabric required will be the total length of one side panel plus the total length of the foot panel. Add extra fabric if you must balance and match stripes, plaids, or large print motifs.

Add the fabric estimates for the top section and the three drop panels together. Divide by 36 (100) to convert this number into yards (meter).

143

To estimate how much ribbon to buy, add twice the finished length of the top section to the finished width, plus 4" (10mm) extra for finishing ends and corners. Divide by 36 (100) to convert this number into yards (meters).

3. Test the fabric for shrinkage and straighten the grain (see CUT-TING FABRIC). Preshrink the ribbon.

4. Cut the fabric for the top section by following step 4 for the basic throw coverlet (see page 136).

Cut the two side panels and the foot panel for the drop to the total length and total width as determined in step 2. Remember to cut these three panels with the lengthwise grain running along the long edges of the panels.

5. If it's necessary to piece the top section, use French seams (see SEAMS).

6. Follow step 6 for the fitted coverlet with flounce, above, to round off the two corners at the foot of the bed on the top section.

7. Narrow hem the head end of the top section (see HEMS) (A).

Pin the ribbon 3" (8cm) in from the sides and foot of the top section, folding the corners in a simple miter (see TRIMS) (B). Fold

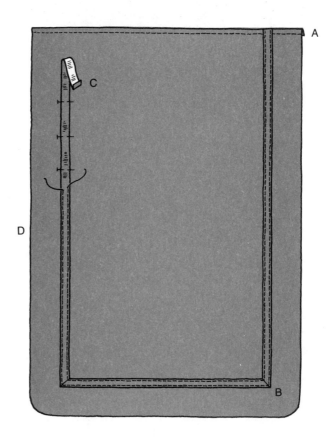

under the raw edges of the ribbon ¼" (6mm) at the hemmed edge of the top (C). Stitch both long edges of the ribbon (D).

8. Stitch the side panels to the foot panel using French seams; press the seam to one side, away from the foot panel (E). Narrow hem the two remaining short edges (F).

Hem one long edge by folding under ¼" (6mm), then turning up 1" (2.5cm). Clip into the seam allowances at the hem fold (G). Topstitch (H) or blindstitch the hem.

9. Right sides together, pin the drop panels to the coverlet top (I). Make a box pleat 5" (12.5cm) deep at each foot corner (J). The seam on the side panel will be on the inside fold of the pleat (K). Baste the pleat in place. Stitch in a ½" (13mm) seam (L).

10. Finish the seam allowances.

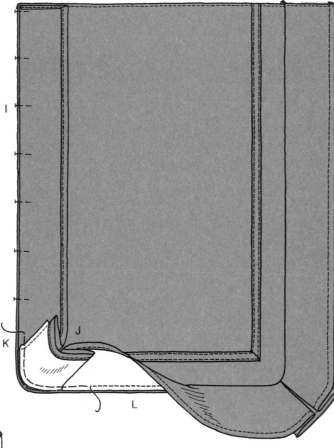

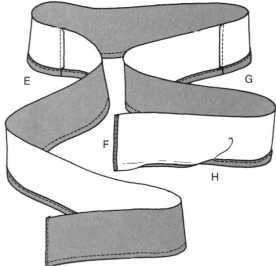

Comforters and Quilts

Comforters are closely related to throw coverlets in terms of how the fabric top and backing are cut and sewn. The major difference is that comforters are filled with multiple layers of fluffy batting and then tied, to anchor all the layers together. Quilts are similar, except that a single layer of batting is used as filler, and the layers are anchored together either with machine quilting or a tying technique called tack quilting.

COMFORTERS

To make tying easier, and to create a nicely puffed-up effect, select a lightweight fabric such as broadcloth, gingham, or muslin for the comforter top and backing. Since it's impossible to press a completed comforter, it's also important to use an easy-care fabric.

You can use the same fabric for the comforter top and backing if you like. Bed sheets are ideal, and an easy way to create a totally matched bed treatment. However, if you use contrasting fabrics, your comforter can be reversed for a quick change of decor. For another kind of coordinated look, you could also use your dust ruffle fabric for the comforter backing, creating a mix-or-match option for dressing your bed.

Basic Comforter Use layers of high-loft polyester batting to pad this luxuriously soft comforter, and narrow ⅛" or 1/16" (3 or 2mm) ribbon to tie the tufts and make the bows.

HOW-TO

1. *Measure the bed (see page 134). Be sure to add about 6" (15cm) to the drop for the "shrinkage" caused by the filler.*

2. *Determine the total width and total length, and estimate the fabric required for the comforter top by following step 2 for the basic throw coverlet (see page 136). Omit the cording and extra fabric for welting.*

The same amount of fabric is required for the comforter backing.

Buy four battings as large as the total width and total length of the comforter top. If you use battings precut for twin, full, queen, or king-size beds, check the label to see if the batting is cut large enough for your comforter as you've measured it.

You'll need approximately 20 yds (19.00m) of ribbon for a twin size comforter, 29 yds (27.65m) for full, 33 yds (31.35m) for queen, and 43 yds (40.85m) for king.

3. *Test the fabric for shrinkage and straighten the grain (see CUTTING FABRIC). Preshrink the ribbon.*

4. *Follow step 4 for the basic throw coverlet to cut the fabric panels for the comforter top and backing.*

5. *If it's necessary to piece the fabric for the top and backing, use plain ⅝" (15mm) seams. Press them open.*

6. *Follow step 7 for the basic throw coverlet to round off the two corners at the foot of the comforter. Round off the corners on the top and backing to match.*

7. *Fold the comforter top into quarters to mark the center on the right side. Use a 12" (31cm) square template to mark the top for tying in a pattern of staggered rows (see* TYING QUILTS AND COMFORTERS*). Use tailor's chalk or erasable marker to mark the top with dots on the right side. Leave a 4" (10cm) border around the edges unmarked.*

8. *Work on a large, flat surface to baste the battings to the comforter backing. Place the backing* **right side down,** *then stack the battings on top. Use a yardstick (meterstick) to stroke away wrinkles from each layer as you stack them.*

Baste the battings to the backing from the center out as if you were preparing to quilt (see QUILTING BY MACHINE*) (A). Baste almost to the edges. Baste the battings to the backing around the edges (B). Trim the battings at the comforter edges to grade the thicknesses (C).*

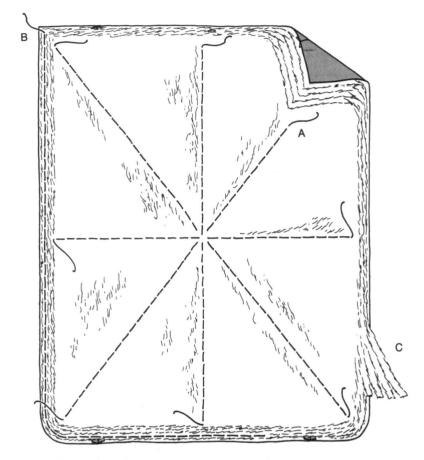

9. *Roll up the backing with the basted battings. Place the comforter top,* right side up, *on your large, flat work surface (D). Unroll the backing, with the backing* right side down *and the battings facing you, over the comforter top. Align the edges of top and backing to match (E). Baste all the layers together around the edges.*

Stitch around the edge, joining the comforter layers in a ⅝" (15mm) seam, and leaving a 36" (92cm) opening at the head end of the comforter for turning (F). Trim the corners diagonally (G), and notch the seam allowances at the curved corners (H). Turn to the right side, and slipstitch the opening closed. Press.

10. *If desired, baste through all thicknesses to prepare for tying.*

Use ribbon to make tufts at each of the marks on the comforter top (see TYING QUILTS AND COMFORTERS*).*

Remove the basting stitches.

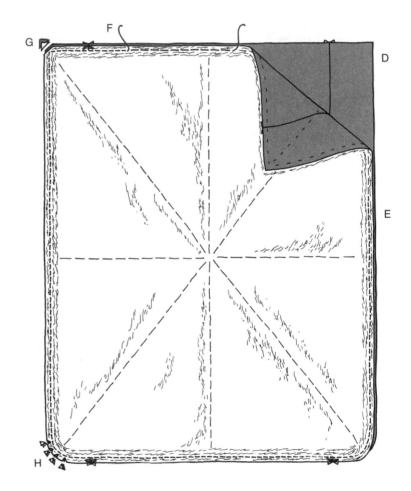

QUILTS

Pieced Crib Quilt Easy strip-piecing makes this quilt top, and the equally easy machine-quilted design traces the straight outlines of the strips. A flock of swan appliqués creates a tranquil scene with a touch of whimsy, one of many possible ways to delight an infant. You might copy a coloring book illustration or trace around cookie cutters to make appliqués for your own version of this quilt. In addition to batting and lightweight fabrics such as broadcloth, polished cotton, muslin, or sheeting, you'll need fusible web for the appliqués, polyester batting, and one skein of black embroidery floss.

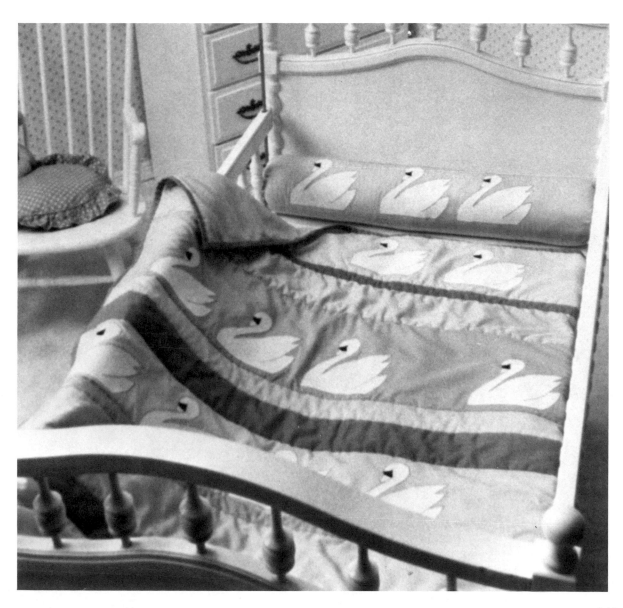

HOW-TO

Note: Use ¼" (6mm) seam allowances.

1. *For a crib quilt about 44" × 59" (112 × 150cm), you'll need the following amounts of 45" (115cm) wide fabric to piece the top and bind the quilt edges: mint green, 1 yd (0.95m); medium blue, ¾ yd (0.70m); light blue, ⅜ yd (0.40m); lavender, ½ yd (0.50m). For the backing, you'll need 1¾ yds (1.60m) of white fabric. For the appliqués, you'll need ½ yd (0.50m) of fabric, 1¼ yds (1.20m) of fusible web, and cardboard or another sturdy material to cut the appliqué template. You'll also need a pre-cut 45" × 60" (114 × 152cm) crib-size polyester batting.*

2. *Test the fabrics for shrinkage and straighten the grain (see* CUTTING FABRIC*).*

3. *Cut crosswise strips 42½" (108cm) long in the following widths: from mint green, one each 9", 7½", 6½", 6", 2½" (23, 19, 16.5, 15, 6.5cm) wide; from medium blue, one each 3½", 2½", 1½" (9, 6.5, 3.8cm) wide; light blue, one each 5⅜", 4½", 1½" (13.6, 11.5, 3.8cm) wide; lavender, one each 9", 4", 1½" (23, 10, 3.8cm) wide.*

From the remaining medium blue fabric, cut 2" (5cm) wide crosswise strips for the quilt binding.

4. *Make a template for the appliqué of your choice (see* TEMPLATES*). Make the appliqué about 5" × 6" (10 × 15cm) in size. Cut 20.*

Stitch appliqués to all the mint green strips except the 2½" (6.5cm) one, and to the 9" (23cm) lavender strip, using the piecing key as a guide for placement (A). (See APPLIQUÉ BY MACHINE*.) Work embroidery on appliqué, using satin stitch (B).*

5. *Stitch the strips together following the piecing key (C). Press the seams toward the upper edge of the quilt.*

6. *Prepare the quilt backing, batting, and top for quilting by basting the layers together, and machine quilt along the seams which join the strips on the quilt top (see* QUILTING BY MACHINE*). Trim the backing and batting even with the edges of the quilt top.*

7. *Join the binding strips together in one long strip; press the seams open. Fold, press, and apply to the edge of the quilt like double-fold bias binding, mitering the corners and finishing the ends (see* BIAS TAPES AND BINDINGS*).*

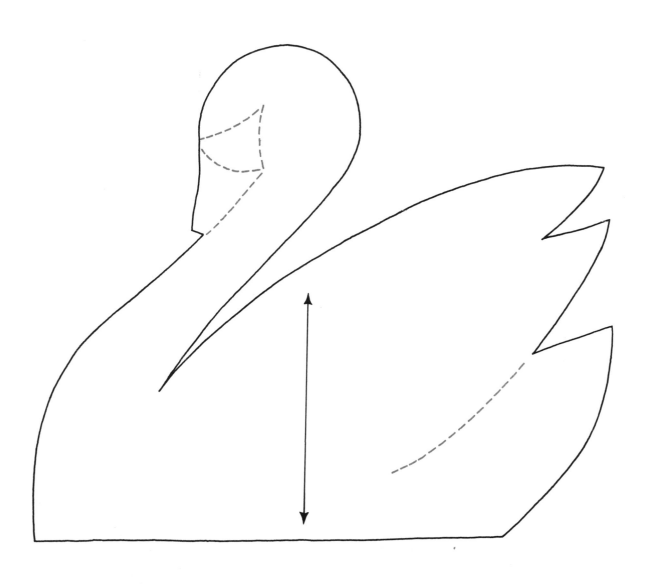

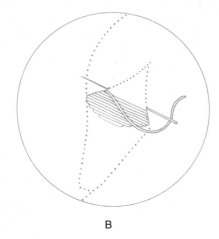

B

C

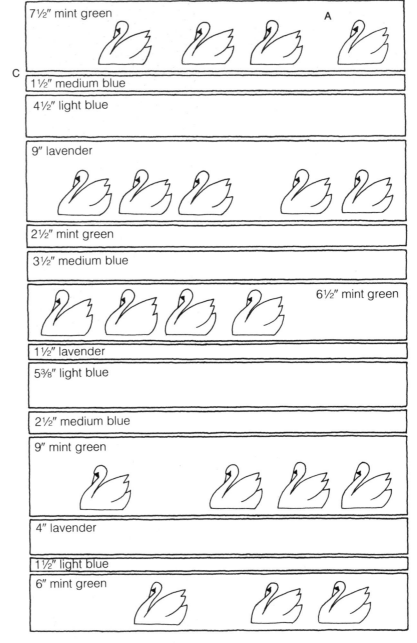

7½" mint green

A

1½" medium blue

4½" light blue

9" lavender

2½" mint green

3½" medium blue

6½" mint green

1½" lavender

5⅜" light blue

2½" medium blue

9" mint green

4" lavender

1½" light blue

6" mint green

Dust Ruffles

These skirts for the box spring give a finished look to your bed treatment. The sewing methods show you how to install the dust ruffle directly onto the box spring, an installation which is as attractive as it is practical. The edge of the dust ruffle is completely hidden under the mattress, it's anchored securely so it won't slip and slide out of place as you make the bed, yet it's easily removed for laundering. Keep in mind that the following two dust ruffles are not suitable for beds with footboards.

Gathered Dust Ruffle In addition to fabric, you'll need snap tape to sew this style of dust ruffle.

HOW-TO

1. *Measure the bed (see page 134).*

2. *Determine the total depth of the dust ruffle by adding 2½" (6.5cm) to the drop. Determine the total length of the dust ruffle by multiplying the finished length by 2 for standard fabric fullness, or by 2½ for a fuller, lush look; multiply by 3 if you're using a sheer fabric.*

Use the estimating formulas for ruffles to determine how many crosswise strips you'll need to cut, and to estimate the fabric required (see RUFFLES*). Allow extra fabric to balance and match stripes, plaids, or large print motifs.*

To determine how much snap tape to buy, add the width of the

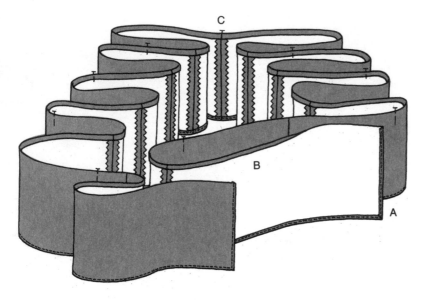

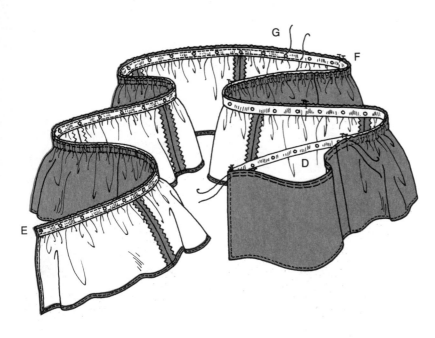

box spring to twice the length, plus 1" (2.5cm) for finishing the ends. Add an extra 1" to 2" (2.5 to 5cm) to allow for shrinkage.

3. *Test the fabric for shrinkage and straighten the grain (see* CUT-TING FABRIC*). Preshrink the snap tape.*

4. *Work on a large, flat surface to mark and cut the fabric. Use a yardstick (meterstick) as a straight edge to help you mark the fabric with cutting lines for the total depth of the crosswise strips—the lengthwise fabric grain runs along the short end of each strip. As you mark, don't include the selvages, which are tightly woven and can cause puckered seams.*

If you're working with a stripe, plaid, or large print motif, be sure to balance the design and match it at the seams; if your fabric has a one-way sheen, texture, or design, use a with-nap cutting plan (see CUTTING FABRIC*).*

5. *Stitch the strips together to form one long strip. Use plain ⅝" (15mm) seams, finish the edges by pinking them, and press the seams open. If your fabric is a sheer, or ravels easily, use French or mock French seams (see* SEAMS*).*

6. *Finish the two short ends and one long edge of the strip with a narrow hem (A) (see* HEMS*).*

7. *Turn under ⅜" (10mm) on the other long edge; press (B). Divide this edge into 10 equal parts using pin markers (C). To gather the strip, use two rows of long machine stitches, a ruffler attachment, or zigzag stitch over a heavy thread (see* GATHERS ON A LARGE SCALE*).*

Divide the snap tape into 10 equal parts with pin markers (D). Pin mark one section of the tape, then unsnap the tape. Turn under ½" (13mm) at the ends of the snap tape (E).

Gather the strip on the marked edge to fit the marked section of the tape, matching the pins (F). Position one edge of the tape even with the folded edge of the ruffle strip; stitch along both long edges of the tape (G), using a zipper foot.

8. Pin the remaining section of snap tape on top of the box spring about ¾" (7.5cm) from the edge. Beginning with a corner at the head of the bed, securely sew both edges of the tape in place by hand (H). Use heavy-duty button and carpet thread and a curved needle, backstitching every 8" to 12" (20.5 to 30.5cm). At the foot corners, hand-gather the tape at the inner edge so it lies flat (I).

Snap the ruffle into place on the box spring.

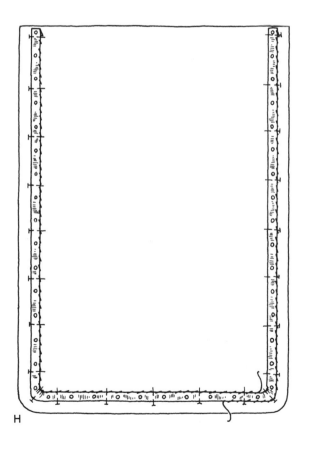

H

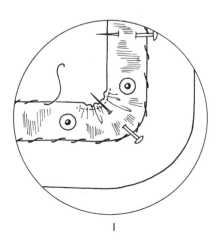

I

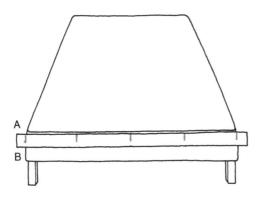

Box-pleated Dust Ruffle When box pleated, a dust ruffle takes on a more tailored character. It's made similarly to the gathered dust ruffle, above, except at the heading. For this dust ruffle, you'll need snap tape in addition to fabric.

HOW-TO

1. *Measure the bed (see page 134).*

2. *Determine the total depth of the dust ruffle by adding 2½" (6.5cm) to the drop for finishing the edges and hems.*

To determine the total length of the dust ruffle, you'll need to plan the spacing of the pleats. Do this for the foot end of the box spring first. Begin with a pleat at each corner of the box spring. Then decide how many pleats you want to make in between these two initial pleats. Count the number of spaces (a space is the distance between two pleats) across the foot of the box spring; including the corner pleats, there will always be one less space than the number of pleats. Divide the width of the box spring (the measurement of the box spring across the foot end) by the number of spaces to determine the measurement of each space.

At this point, it helps to make a guide from a strip of paper about 3" (7.5cm) wide (adding machine paper is ideal). Mark on it the spaces between the pleats for the foot end of the bed (A). Each mark represents one pleat. Hold the paper guide up to the box spring to check the accuracy of your pleat spacing (B). Adjust the spacing if necessary and make new marks.

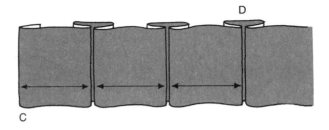

D

C

Use this paper guide to estimate the number of pleats you'll need to make on each side of the box spring. Just plan to space the pleats the same distance apart as on the foot of the bed. At each head corner of the box spring, do not plan to make an entire pleat. This edge of the dust ruffle can be left flat and unpleated, or turned under in a half-pleat (C), to compensate for any adjustment needed in the pleat spacing for the sides of the dust ruffle.

Next, decide how deep you want to make the pleats—about 2" (5cm) deep is a good rule of thumb. To make a box pleat, you'll fold two pleats so they meet (D), so to find the fabric allowance for each box pleat, multiply the pleat depth (E) by 4. For example, if you're folding the pleats 2" (5cm) deep, the fabric allowance is 8" (20.5cm) per box pleat.

To find the total pleat allowance, multiply the total number of pleats × the fabric allowance per pleat. Then, to find the total length of the dust ruffle, add the following:

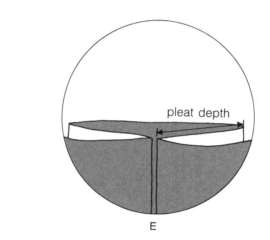

pleat depth

E

Total Pleat Allowance _____

+ Width of Box Spring _____

+ Twice the Length of Box Spring _____

+ 7" (18cm) for Folding and Hemming
the Head-of-the-Bed Edges _____

Total Length of Dust Ruffle _____

Another Way to Pleat Dust Ruffles

If you prefer a more tailored look than all-over box pleats for your dust ruffle, make just a few pleats. Plan to make a box pleat at each foot corner of the box spring, and a half box pleat at each head corner. If you like, you can also center a single box pleat in between each of these initial pleats.

You'll require less fabric than if making all-over box pleats, although you should make each box pleat deeper for the dust ruffle to drape smoothly. Add 12″ to 20″ (30.5 to 51cm) of fabric per box pleat to determine the total length of the dust ruffle when estimating the fabric requirements.

3. *To estimate the fabric required, first find out how many crosswise strips of fabric will be needed. To do this, divide the total length of the dust ruffle by the fabric width (minus the selvages and 1¼″ [3.2cm] for seam allowances). If this number does not come out evenly, round it off to the next highest whole number.*

Then multiply the number of crosswise strips of fabric × the total depth of the ruffle. This gives you the basic fabric estimate. Allow extra fabric if you're working with a stripe, plaid, or large print motif which must be balanced and matched at the seams. Divide this number by 36 (100) to convert it into yards (meters).

To estimate the amount of snap tape you'll need, add the width of the box spring to twice the length, then add 1″ (2.5cm) for finishing the ends. Add an extra 1″ to 2″ (2.5 to 5cm) to allow for shrinkage.

4. *Test the fabric for shrinkage and straighten the grain (see* CUTTING FABRIC*). Preshrink the snap tape.*

5. *Follow steps 4, 5, and 6 for the gathered dust ruffle, above, to cut and piece the fabric strips, and to hem the side and bottom edges. Try to position the seams so they'll be hidden inside pleats.*

6. *Turn under the remaining long edge of the ruffle strip ⅜″ (10mm) and press. Mark the midpoint of the ruffle strip, and the midpoint of your paper guide from step 2.*

Matching the midpoints of the ruffle strip and your paper guide, fold the pleats according to the spacing and pleat allowance you've decided upon. Baste the pleats in place along the upper edge.

7. *Unsnap the sections of snap tape. Turn under the raw edges of each section ½″ (13mm).*

Place the edge of one tape section along the folded upper edge of the ruffle strip, covering the raw edge of the strip (F). Stitch close to both long edges of the tape (G), using a zipper foot.

8. *Snap the tape sections together. Place the dust ruffle on top of the box spring about ¾″ (20mm) in from the edge. Pin the unstitched section of the tape to the box spring, then carefully unsnap the tape sections.*

Securely sew both edges of the tape to the box spring, following step 8 for the gathered dust ruffle, above.

Snap the dust ruffle into place on the box spring.

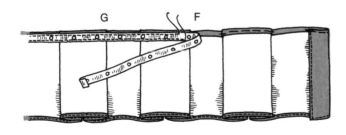

Pillows

Pillows, associated as they are with comfort, help to make a room warm and inviting. As small sewing projects, they're the perfect way to introduce a spot of color, texture, or print quickly into a room. If you have the time and want to make a bigger change, sometimes all you have to do is make a mass of pillows. Group them in graduated sizes on the bed, arrange them artfully to disguise a time-worn sofa, or cover great foam squares and replace that sofa altogether with modular pillow seating units.

Though it seems as if there are countless kinds of pillows, there are only two basic types. Knife-edge pillows are plump in the center, and taper off in thickness at the sides. It takes just a plain seam to join the pillow cover front and back at the sides, and this seam is often decorated with trim. Box-edge pillows are evenly plump from the center to the sides. To give a box-edge pillow cover side depth, there may be gathers at the corners, or an inserted section called a boxing strip at the sides.

Both knife-edge and box-edge pillow covers are featured on the following pages, with basic styles and their variations included in each category. In addition, there are methods for making bed pillow shams, which are special-purpose knife-edge pillow covers for the finishing touch on a bed treatment.

PILLOW FORMS

Most of the pillow projects on the following pages are designed to fit ready-made forms in standard sizes. Unless you require an odd pillow size or shape, it's easier and usually more economical to use a purchased pillow form as a filler than to make your own form. The fabric amounts given are approximate. For pillows with ruffles, the ruffles are cut crosswise to use the fabric economically. If you prefer to cut the ruffles lengthwise, to use fabric which has a special design motif, or to use another pillow form size, adapt the how-to's by adjusting the fabric estimates and cut sizes of the cover sections.

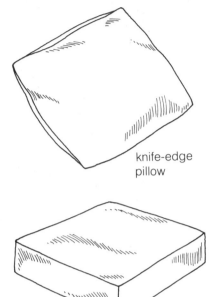

knife-edge pillow

box-edge pillow

CLOSURES FOR PILLOW COVERS

An easy-to-open closure on the back of a pillow cover is a practical convenience because the pillow form inside can be removed in an instant when it's time to launder or dry-clean the cover. A plain *sham closing* is traditional for decorative bed pillow cases. *Zippers inserted in seams* are especially suitable for pillow covers which are fitted snugly. A *slipstitched seam* is by far the most inconspicuous closure, and is often used on toss pillows. However, the hand stitches must be picked out and resewn each time the pillow form is removed.

Knife-edge Pillow Covers

Use crisp, firmly woven fabrics which are medium to heavyweight for the best pillow covers. Chintz, sateen, linen weaves, woolens, synthetic suede, raw silk, piqué, duck, and sheeting work especially well. If you've selected a soft or lightweight fabric, quilt it or back it with a layer of fusible interfacing to add body and crisp support.

Basic Cover At its most basic level, a knife-edge pillow cover is two fabric squares sewn together. This method shows you how to make a cover with a slip-stitched closure, the fastest and least conspicuous technique. It's an easy way to make a beautiful pillow cover, and is especially suitable if you're working with a unique fabric. Besides the fabrics recommended above, you could also use a portion of an antique quilt, a hand-loomed ethnic fabric, or needlework such as appliqué or embroidery to cover pillows in this way.

HOW-TO

Note: Use ½″ (13mm) seam allowances.

1. *To cover a 16″ (40.5cm)*

Crisp Corners

To help the corners of a pillow cover keep their shape, fuse a piece of interfacing to the wrong side of one cover section at each corner before sewing the sections together.

Pleasingly Plump Pillows

It takes a tightly fitted cover to make pillows look as smooth and plump as they appear in decorating books and magazines. To achieve that picture-perfect snug fit, make the cover smaller than the measurement of the form. Just use deeper seam allowances than the sewing how-to's suggest—use ⅝" or even ¾" (15 or 20mm) instead of ½" (13mm) for example. This is especially important if you're covering a foam form. Foam compresses considerably, and a tight fit is the only way to create a wrinkle-free cover.

square form, you'll need about ½ yd (0.50m) of any width fabric.

To cover a 20" (51cm) square form, you'll need about 1¼ yds (1.20m) of 35" (90cm) wide fabric, or about ⅝ yd (0.60m) of 45", 54", or 60" (115, 140, or 150cm) wide fabric.

Allow extra fabric if working with stripes, plaids, or prints which must be centered and matched at the seams (see CUTTING FABRIC).

2. Test the fabric for shrinkage and straighten the grain (see CUTTING FABRIC).

3. Cut two 17" (43cm) square sections to cover the 16" (40.5cm) form.

Cut two 21" (53.5cm) square sections to cover the 20" (51cm) form.

4. With right sides matching, pin the two cover sections together. Stitch, leaving a large opening at the center of one side

(A). Leave an 11" (27.9cm) opening for the 16" (40.5cm) size, and a 15" (38cm) opening for the 20" (51cm) size.

5. Turn to the right side, through the opening. Don't trim the corners or grade the seams before turning the cover unless your fabric is bulky. Leaving the seam allowance intact helps to strengthen the edges of the pillow cover and fill out the corners.

Insert the form. Slipstitch the opening closed (see HAND STITCHES).

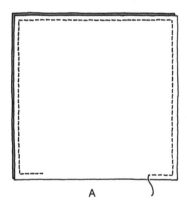

A

The Zippered Pillow Cover

If you prefer to use a zipper as a closure on your pillow cover, cut the cover back section 1¼" (3.2cm) wider than the front. Then cut the cover back into two sections about 2" (5cm) from one edge. Baste these two back sections together in a ⅝" (15mm) seam; insert the zipper in this seam (B). Positioning the zipper to one side makes the closure less noticeable, and since it's applied away from the seamline, it won't interfere with any trims inserted in the seams.

B

Cover with Ribbon Trim Grosgrain ribbon is a smart, tailored trim for pillow covers, but any kind of band trim including galloon lace or flat braid could be used to accent your decorating scheme.

HOW-TO

Note: Use ½" (13mm) seam allowances.

1. *Use the same fabric estimates as given in step 1 for the basic cover, above. For the 16" (40.5cm) form, you'll need about 1½ yds (1.40cm) of ⅞" (22mm) ribbon; for the 20" (51cm) form, you'll need about 2 yds (1.90m).*

2. *Test the fabric for shrinkage and straighten the grain (see* CUTTING FABRIC*). Preshrink the ribbon.*

3. *Follow step 3 for the basic cover (see page 162) to cut the fabric.*

4. *On one fabric section, mark a trim placement line 2" (5cm) from the edges (A). Beginning at one corner, pin the ribbon along the placement line. Fold the corners in a simple miter. Where the ribbon ends meet, fold over one ribbon edge to form the last miter. Stitch both edges of the trim all around.*

5. *Follow steps 4 and 5 for the basic cover, above, to complete the pillow cover.*

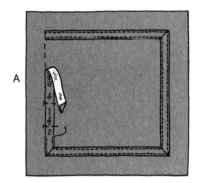

A

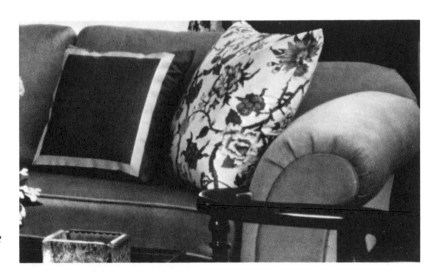

Cover with Welting Trim Welting is a classic trim for knife-edge pillow covers, but you can use this same sewing method to insert other trims such as lace or a self-fabric ruffle in the cover seam if you prefer.

HOW-TO

Note: Use ½" (13mm) seam allowances.

1. *To cover a 16" (40.5cm) square form, you'll need about 1⅛ yds (1.10m) of 35" or 45" (90 or 115cm) wide fabric, or about ⅞ yd (0.80m) of 54" or 60" (140 or 150cm) wide fabric; plus 2 yds (1.90m) of ⅜" (10mm) piping cord.*

To cover a 20" (51cm) square form, you'll need about 2 yds (1.85m) of 35" or 45" (90 or 115cm) wide fabric, or about 1¼ yds (1.15m) of 54" or 60" (140 or 150cm) wide fabric; plus about 2½ yds (2.30cm) of ⅜" (10mm) piping cord.

Allow extra fabric if working with stripes, plaids, or prints which must be centered and matched at the seams (see CUTTING LAYOUTS).

2. Test the fabric for shrinkage and straighten the grain (see CUTTING FABRIC).

3. Follow step 3 for the basic cover (see page 162) to cut fabric for the cover sections.

4. From the remaining fabric, cut bias strips 2½" (6.5cm) wide and cover the cord to make welting (see WELTING).

5. Beginning at the center of one side, pin the welting to the edge of one section of the cover, on the right side (A). Place the welting stitching ½" (15mm) from the cut edge of the cover section.

Clip into the welting seam allowance to turn the corners (B), and trim the welting where the ends meet for an overlap seam.

Use a zipper foot to baste the welting to the cover section.

6. Follow steps 4 and 5 for the basic cover to complete the pillow cover, using a zipper foot and following the welting basting to stitch the seam.

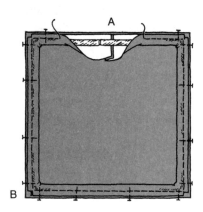

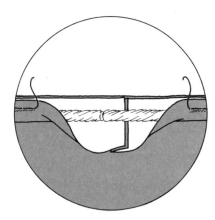

Cover with Headed Ruffle This self-fabric ruffle trim is stitched to the pillow cover top, rather than inserted in the seams, so both sides of the ruffle form a decorative edge.

HOW-TO

Note: Use ½" (13mm) seam allowances. Ruffle strips are cut crosswise.

1. *To cover a 14" (35cm) square form, you'll need about 1 yd (0.95m) of 35" or 45" (90 or 115cm) wide fabric, or about ¾ yd (10.70m) of 54" or 60" (140 or 150cm) wide fabric.*

Allow extra fabric if working with stripes, plaids, or prints which must be centered and matched at the seams (see CUTTING LAYOUTS*).*

2. *Test the fabric for shrinkage and straighten the grain (see* CUTTING FABRIC*).*

3. *Cut two 15" (38cm) square sections for the pillow cover. Use the full width of your fabric to cut the ruffle strips. Each strip is 3½" (9cm) wide. Cut 5 strips of 35" (90cm) fabric or 4 strips of 45" (115cm), or 3 strips of 54" or 60" (140 or 150cm).*

4. *On the right side of one cover section, mark a ruffle placement line 1" (2.5cm) from all edges (A). This will be the top of the cover.*

5. *Join the ruffle strips with French seams (see* SEAMS*) into one continuous ruffle strip. Finish both long edges with narrow hems (see* HEMS*).*

Use long machine stitches ½" (13mm) and ⅝" (15mm) from one long edge to gather the ruffle.

Use pins to divide the ruffle into 4 equal sections. Pin the ruf-

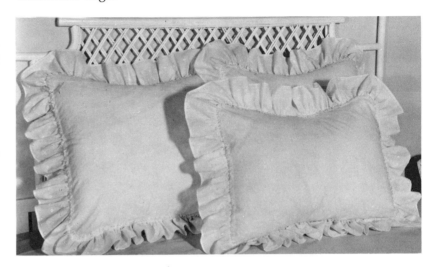

fle to the placement line on the cover top, positioning a pin marker on the ruffle at each corner of the cover top. Center the rows of gathering stitches over the placement line, and arrange the gathers into even folds. Ease in extra ruffle fullness at the corners so the ruffle lies flat.

Stitch the ruffle to the cover top between the rows of gathering stitches.

6. *Follow steps 4 and 5 for the basic cover to complete the pillow top, leaving an opening 7" (18cm) long on one edge and folding the ruffle toward the center of the cover so it's not caught in the seam.*

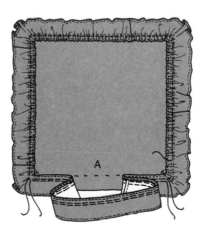

Tufted Pillows Trim these knife-edge pillows with a matching or contrasting ruffle. Covered buttons are used to make the central tuft—forms to cover the buttons come in a handy kit, with instructions.

HOW-TO

Note: Use ½" (13mm) seam allowances. Ruffle strips are cut crosswise.

1. To make a 16" (41cm) square pillow with contrasting ruffle, you'll need about ½ yd (0.50m) of any width fabric for the cover. For the contrasting ruffle, you'll need about ¾ yd (0.70m) of 35" or 45" (90 or 115cm) wide fabric, or about ½ yd of 54" or 60" (140 or 150cm) wide fabric. To fill the cover, you'll need 1 lb (450g) of polyester fiberfill.

To make a 24" (61cm) square pillow with matching ruffle, you'll need about 3⅛ yds

(2.90m) of 35" (90cm) wide fabric, 2⅜ yds (2.20m) of 45" (115cm) wide fabric, or 2 yds (1.85m) of 54" or 60" (140 or 150cm) wide fabric. To fill the cover, you'll need 2 lbs (900 g.) of polyester fiberfill.

For each pillow, you'll need two 1¼" (3.2cm) button forms.

Allow extra fabric if working with stripes, plaids, or large prints which must be centered and matched at the seams (see CUTTING LAYOUTS).

2. Test the fabric for shrinkage and straighten the grain (see CUT-TING FABRIC).

3. For the 16" (41cm) pillow, cut two 17" (43cm) squares for the cover sections. From contrast fabric, cut the following number of 4" (10cm) wide crosswise ruffle strips: 6 of 35" (90cm) wide fabric; 5 of 45" (115cm); 4 of 54" (140cm); or 3 of 60" (150cm).

For the 24" (61cm) pillow, cut two 25" (63.5cm) squares for the cover sections, and the following number of 7" (18cm) wide crosswise ruffle strips: 9 of 35" (90cm) wide fabric; 7 of 45" (115cm); 6 of 54" (140cm); or 5 of 60" (150cm).

Reserve the fabric scraps for covering the buttons.

4. *Stitch the ruffle strips to-gether to form one continuous strip. Fold the strip in half along its length, wrong sides together. Press.*

Divide the ruffle into fourths and mark with pins (A). Use long machine stitches ½" (13mm) and ¾" (20mm) from the raw edges to gather the ruffle.

Pin the ruffle to the right side of one cover section, with the raw edges even. Match a pin marker on the ruffle to each corner of the cover. Gather the ruffle to fit. Arrange the gathers evenly and ease in extra gathers at the corners. Baste the ruffle to the cover.

5. *Follow steps 4 and 5 for the basic cover (see page 162) to complete the project, leaving a 6" (15cm) opening on one side for turning.*

After turning, fill the pillow firmly through the opening before slipstitching the opening closed.

6. *Cover the button forms with fabric, following the button manufacturer's instructions. With one length of thread, sew a button to the center of each side of the pillow; pull the thread tightly to form the tufted center. Secure the thread with small stitches underneath one button.*

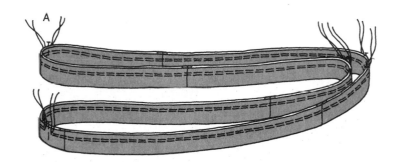

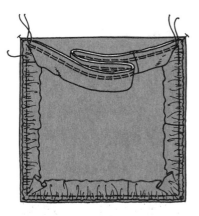

Tie-on Covers Use two coordinating fabrics for this layered pillow cover—one fabric to make the pillow form, and one for the tie-on outer cover.

HOW-TO

Note: Use ½" (13mm) seam allowances.

1. *To cover a 16" (40.5cm) square form, you'll need about ½ yd (0.50m) of any width fabric. For the tie-on outer cover, you'll need about 1 yd (0.95m) of 35" or 45" (90 or 115cm) wide fabric, or about ¾ yd (0.70m) of 54" or 60" (140 or 150cm) wide fabric.*

To cover a 20" × 26" (51 × 66cm) standard bed pillow, you'll need about ¾ yd (0.70m) of 45" (115cm) wide fabric or about ⅝ yd (0.60) of 54" or 60" (140 or 150cm) wide fabric. For the tie-on outer cover, you'll need about 1¾ yds (1.60m) of 45" (115cm) wide fabric or about 1¼ yds (1.15m) of 54" or 60" (140 or 150cm) wide fabric.

Allow extra fabric if working with stripes, plaids, or prints which must be centered and matched at the seams (see CUTTING FABRIC*).*

2. *Test the fabric for shrinkage and straighten the grain (see* CUTTING FABRIC*).*

3. *To cover the square form, follow steps 3 through 5 for the basic cover (see page 162).*

To cover the bed pillow, cut two 21" × 27" (53.5 × 68.5cm) fabric sections; follow steps 4 and 5 for the basic cover, leaving a 20" (51cm) opening.

4. *For the tie-on cover to fit the square form, cut the following sections: two 17" × 15" (43 × 38cm) covers; four 17" × 2½"*

(43 × 7cm) facings; two 22" × 5" (56 × 12.5cm) ruffles; and eight 13" × 2½" (33 × 7cm) ties.

For the tie-on cover to fit the bed pillow, cut the following sections: two 21" × 25" (53.5 × 63.5cm) covers; four 21" × 2½" (53.5 × 7cm) facings; two 37" × 5" (94 × 10cm) ruffles; and eight 16" × 2½" (40.5 × 7cm) ties.

5. For each tie-on cover, make eight ties (see TIES, DRAWSTRINGS, AND LOOPS).

Pin four ties to the right side of each cover section 4" (10cm) from the center of the 17¼" (44cm) edge for the square pillow, or the 21" (53.5cm) edge for the bed pillow; baste the ties in place (A).

6. Turn under ¼" (6mm) on one long edge of each facing section; press. Stitch next to the fold.

Right sides together, pin the facings to each cover section, over the basted ties. Stitch the seams. Press each seam toward the facing.

7. Fold each ruffle in half along its length, with right sides together. Stitch the short ends. Trim the seams, and turn the ruffle to the right side; press.

Use long machine stitches to prepare the ruffle for gathering (see RUFFLES). Gather the ruffle to fit between the facings of one cover section; baste the ruffles in place (B).

8. Right sides together, pin the pillow cover sections, matching the seamlines at the facings; stitch, continuing across the facings. Press seams open (C).

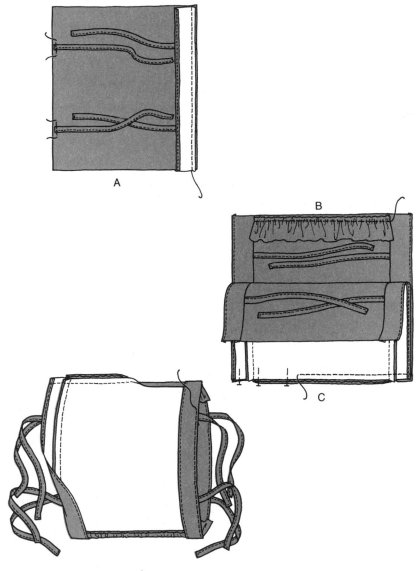

Fold the facings to the wrong side of the cover, and press. Stitch close to each faced edge, beginning and ending at each ruffle.

Turn the cover right side out. Insert the covered pillow form, and tie the outer cover in place at each side.

169

Shams

Shams are decorative covers for bed pillows, and are distinguished by the overlapping closure on the back. Make them to match your sheets, the bed covering, a comforter, or use deluxe satins and laces to create a luxurious boudoir look.

Sham with Flanged Edge This easy variation of the basic sham is cut extra-wide so a row of topstitching is all you need to create the flat, flange border.

HOW-TO

Note: Use ½" (13mm) seam allowances. Fabric estimates are for one sham.

1. *For a standard size, you'll need about 2¼ yds (2.10m) of 35" (90cm) wide fabric, or about 1½ yds (1.40m) of 45", 54", or 60" (115, 140, or 150cm) wide fabric.*

For a queen size, you'll need fabric at least 45" (115cm) wide—about 1½ yds (1.40m) of 45", 54", or 60" (115, 140, or 150cm) wide fabric.

For a king size, you'll need fabric at least 45" (115cm) wide—about 2¼ yds (2.10m) of 45" (115cm) wide fabric, or about

1¾ yds (1.60m) of 54" or 60" (140 or 150cm) wide fabric.

For a European size, you'll need about 1¾ yds (1.60m) of any width fabric.

Allow extra fabric if working with stripes, plaids, or prints which must be centered and matched at the seams (see CUTTING FABRIC).

2. Test the fabric for shrinkage and straighten the grain (see CUTTING FABRIC).

3. Cut one sham front and two sham backs for your pillow size:

4. On each back section, narrow hem one short edge (see HEMS). Right sides up, lap the right half over the left half about 3¾" (9.5cm) (A) until the back matches the front in size; baste (B).

5. With right sides matching, pin the sham front and back together; stitch. Trim diagonally across the corners, then turn right side out. Press.

6. On the right side, topstitch 2½" (6.5cm) from all edges (C).

SIZE	FRONT (CUT 1)	BACK (CUT 2)
Standard	26" × 32" (66 × 81cm)	26" × 18½" (66 × 47cm)
Queen	26" × 36" (66 × 89cm)	26" × 20½" (66 × 52cm)
King	26" × 42" (66 × 106.5cm)	26" × 23½" (66 × 59.5cm)
European	30" × 30" (76 × 76cm)	30" × 17½" (76 × 44.5cm)

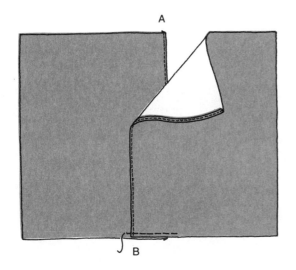

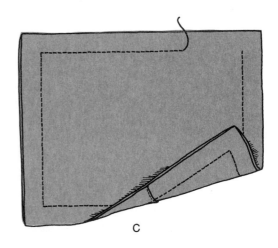

Box-edge Pillow Covers

Box-edge pillows offer true comfort for seating or padding the back of a chair, so they can be functional as well as decorative. As for knife-edge covers, it's best to select a crisp, firmly woven fabric so the pillow cover keeps its shape nicely.

Floor Cushions Cover large foam squares with a sturdy fabric to make tie-together floor cushions. The how-to shows you how to make one, but you can make as many as you like and stack them or tie them together as needed.

HOW-TO

Note: Use ½" (13mm) seam allowances.

1. *To cover a 24" (61cm) square foam form 7" (18cm) deep, you'll need about 2½ yds (2.30m) of 35" (90cm) wide fabric; about 2¼ yds (2.10m) of 45" (115cm) wide fabric; or about 1⅝ yds (1.50m) of 54" or 60" (140 or 150cm) wide fabric. Allow extra fabric if working with stripes, plaids, or prints which must be centered and matched at the seams (see CUTTING FABRIC). You'll also need two 18" (45cm) zippers.*

2. Test the fabric for shrinkage and straighten the grain (see CUT-TING FABRIC).

3. Cut two 25" (63.5cm) squares for the cover front and back sections. Cut eight 2½" × 10" (6.5 × 25cm) ties. Cut three sections for the boxing strip—one 8" × 54" (20.5 × 137cm), and two 4½" × 44" (11.5 × 112cm) strips for the zippers. If using 35" or 45" (90 or 115cm) wide fabric, these boxing strip sections will have to be pieced. Remember to allow extra fabric for seam allowances.

4. Right sides together, stitch the two boxing strip sections for the zippers on the long edges, leaving a 36" (91.5m) opening at the center of the seam (A). Baste the opening closed, and press the seam open.

Center the zippers over the basted opening so the zipper pulls meet. Insert the zippers (B), using a zipper foot. Remove the basting stitches.

Stitch the zipper strip to the remaining boxing strip section to make one continuous boxing strip (C).

5. Make eight ties (see TIES, DRAW-STRINGS, AND LOOPS).

6. On the right side, baste a tie 1¾" (4.5cm) from each corner of one pillow cover section (D). This section will be the front of the pillow cover.

7. Carefully pin the boxing strip to the front cover section. Position the strip so that the zipper pulls meet at the center of one side of the pillow cover. Mark the corners. Unpin the boxing strip, and mark the corners on the other edge of the boxing strip. Stitch ½" (13mm) from the edge through each mark for about ½" (13mm) on each side of each mark (E).

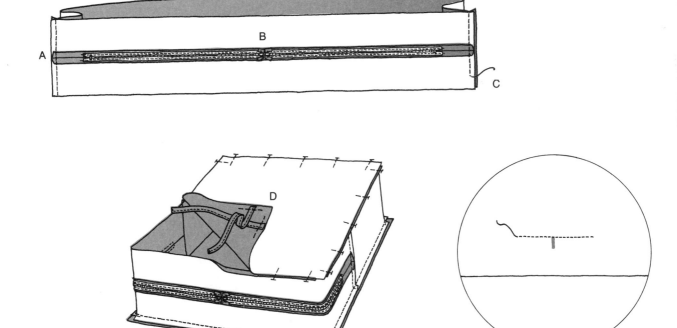

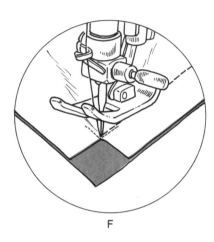

F

With right sides together, pin the boxing strip to the front cover section, matching the markings on the boxing strip to the cover corners. Stitch; at each corner, stop stitching and clip the boxing strip seam allowance to turn the corner (F).

Open up one of the zippers to provide an opening for turning. Stitch the boxing strip to the back cover section as described above for the front cover section.

8. Turn the cover right side out. Open the zippers to insert the pillow form.

Bolster Pillows with Duffle Covers Make custom bolster forms in two sizes, then sew coordinated drawstring covers. As a fine detail, the facings and drawstrings are cut from the same fabric used to cover the form.

HOW-TO

Note: Use ½" (13mm) seam allowances.

1. *For the small, 18" (46cm) long pillow, you'll need about 1⅛ yds (1.05m) of 45", 54", or 60" (115, 140, or 150cm) wide fabric for the bolster form, facings, and drawstrings; about ⅝ yd (0.60m) of 45", 54", or 60" (115, 140, or 150cm) wide contrasting fabric for the cover; and 1 lb (450g) of polyester fiberfill.*

For the large, 36" (92cm) long pillow, you'll need about 1½ yds (1.40m) of 45", 54", or 60" (115, 140, or 150cm) wide fabric for the bolster form, facings, and drawstrings; about 1⅛ yds (1.10m) of 45", 54", or 60" (115, 140, or 150cm) wide fabric for the cover; and 2 lbs (900g) of polyester fiberfill.

Allow extra fabric if working with stripes, plaids, or prints which must be centered and matched at the seams (see CUTTING FABRIC*).*

2. *Test the fabric for shrinkage and straighten the grain (see* CUTTING FABRIC*).*

3. *From bolster fabric, cut one 16" × 37" (40.5 × 94cm) section for the small pillow, or one 31" × 37" (78.5 × 94cm) section for the large pillow. For each pillow, cut from bolster fabric*

two facings 3¾" × 37½" (9.5 × 95cm), two drawstrings 2½" × 41½" (6.5 × 105cm), and two circles 8" (20.5cm) in diameter for end sections.

From contrasting fabric, cut one 19" × 37½" (48 × 95cm) cover section for the small pillow, or one 37" × 37" (95 × 95cm) cover section for the large pillow.

4. *For the bolster form, make a row of long machine stitches for gathering ½" and ¼" (13 and 6mm) from each long edge of the bolster section. Begin and end the stitches ½" (13mm) from the short edges (A).*

Right sides together, fold the bolster section in half across its length. Stitch, leaving an opening for turning (B).

Gather the long edges of the bolster to fit each end section. Distribute the gathers evenly, and stitch (C).

5. Turn right side out. Insert the fiberfill through the opening. Slipstitch the opening closed (see HAND STITCHES).

6. For the cover, turn under ¼" (6mm) on each long edge of each facing; press. Right sides together, pin a facing to each long edge of the small pillow or to two opposite edges of the large pillow cover; stitch. Press each seam toward the facing.

Right sides together, fold the cover in half across its length and pin the edges together. Stitch, leaving a 1¼" (3.2cm) opening 4¾" (12cm) from each end (D). Press the seam open.

Turn the cover right side out.

7. Fold the facings down to the inside. Press. To form the casings for the drawstrings, stitch on the lower edge of the facings and again 1¼" (3.2cm) away (E).

8. Make two drawstrings (see TIES, DRAWSTRINGS, AND LOOPS). Insert a drawstring in each casing, through the opening.

Slip the bolster form into the cover; pull the drawstrings and tie the ends.

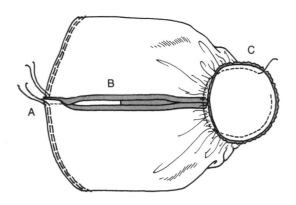

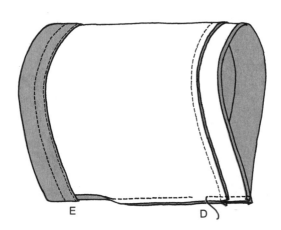

Basic Cover with Turkish Corners These gathered corners have also been dubbed "kissing corners," after the puckered fullness which gives this cover its side depth.

HOW-TO

Note: Use ½" (13mm) seam allowances.

1. To cover a 16" (40.5cm) pillow form with a 4" (10cm) side depth, you'll need about 1¼ yds (1.20m) of 35" (90cm) wide fabric, or about ¾ yd (0.70m) of 45", 54", or 60" (115, 140, or 150cm) wide fabric. Allow extra fabric if working with stripes, plaids, or prints which must be centered and matched at the seams (see CUTTING FABRIC).

2. Test the fabric for shrinkage and straighten the grain (see CUTTING FABRIC).

3. Cut two 21" (53.5cm) squares for the cover sections.

4. Mark each cover section 3½" (9cm) from each corner (A).

Using a cup or glass as a template, round off all the corners to match (B).

Make two rows of long machine stitches ½" (13mm) from the edge and ⅛" (3mm) from the edge (C). Gather each corner between the marks. Gather the corners evenly so the distance between each set of marks is 3" (7.5cm) (D).

5. With right sides together and corner marks matching, pin the cover sections together. Stitch, leaving an 11" (27.9cm) opening at the center of one side for turning.

Turn right side out. Insert the pillow form, and slipstitch the opening closed.

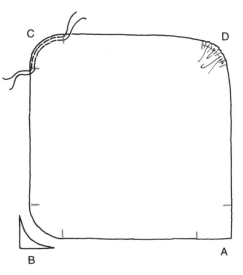

Cover with Turkish Corners and Welting Cover jumbo piping cord with contrasting fabric to accent the side seams in this variation of the basic Turkish corner style.

HOW-TO

Note: Use ½" (13mm) seam allowances.

1. *Use the fabric estimates given in step 1 for the basic cover with Turkish corners (see page 176). You'll need about ¾ yd (0.70m) of contrast fabric to cover 2 yds (1.90m) of ¾" (20mm) piping cord.*

2. *Test the fabric for shrinkage and straighten the grain (see* CUTTING FABRIC*).*

3. *Follow steps 3 and 4 for the basic cover to cut the sections and gather the corners.*

4. *Cut bias strips 3½" (9cm) wide and cover the piping cord to make welting (see* WELTING*).*

5. *Pin the welting to the right side of one cover section, clipping the welting seam allowance at the corners. Join the ends in an overlapping seam; baste, using a zipper foot.*

6. *Follow step 5 for the basic cover to finish, using a zipper foot and following the previous welting basting to stitch the seam.*

Table Coverings and Accessories

If you have a definite decorating scheme in mind, or a table that doesn't conform to ready-made cloth sizes, making your own table coverings is an excellent project. Covering a table involves shaping the edges of a flat panel of fabric to echo the outline of the tabletop, then adding a hem or other edge finish. With variations in trims, and the creative options offered by layering tablecloths, you can use table coverings in a great many ways.

These pages feature the following kinds of projects for table treatments:

- Tablecloths for round, oval, rectangular, and square tables.

- Accessories such as napkins, placemats, and table runners.

Tablecloths

Whether you're covering a table for bedside, living room, kitchen, or formal dining room, there's a broad range of suitable fabrics. For dining, set a traditional table with damask and other jacquard weave fabrics, fine linen weaves in pure linen or easy-care fiber blends, piqué, or lace layered over a richly colored plain cloth. In a more casual mood, use gingham, calico, printed broadcloth, batik, or chintz. Next to a bed or a chair, a table long past its prime can get a new lease on life with a full-length tablecloth cut from fabric matched to the curtains, the cushions, or other fabric furnishings in the room.

When making tablecloths, there's one cardinal rule— use the widest fabric possible to keep seams to a minimum. Bed sheets, because of their generous widths and attractive fabric designs, are especially popular for large tablecloths.

MEASURING TABLES

Use a yardstick (meterstick) or folding metal ruler to measure your table. If measuring a dining table, you'll need one of the dining chairs, too.

Measure the length and width of the tabletop first. For *rectangular* tables, measure the length and width along the sides of the tabletop. For *square* tables, measure just one side, for the length and width are equal. For *round* tables, measure the diameter across the tabletop. For *oval* tables, measure the length and width at the widest points of the oval.

Also measure the *drop*—the distance from the edge of the table to where you want the finished hem of the tablecloth to fall. For dining, the standard drop ends about 6" (15cm) above the chair seat so it clears the diner's lap. For floor-length cloths, measure the drop from the table to the carpeting; or plan for an extra-long cloth that drapes gracefully on the floor for an extravagantly sweeping hem.

Use the formulas below to estimate how much fabric to buy.

Estimating Fabric for Tablecloths

1. Determine the total width by adding twice the drop to the width or diameter of the table, plus 1¼" (3.2cm) to allow for narrow hems or seam allowances for trims. If bias binding is used as a finish, no hem or seam allowance is required.

Width or Diameter of Table _____

+ Twice the Drop _____

+ 1¼" (3.2cm) for Hem or
Seam Allowance, if Required _____

_ _ _ _ _ _ _ _

Total Width of Tablecloth _____

2. Divide the total width by the fabric width (minus selvages and minus 1¼" [3.2cm] seam allowances) to determine the total number of full fabric-width panels needed. If the number of panels does not come out evenly, round off to the next highest whole number. Most tablecloths require 1 or 2 panels.

$$\frac{\text{Total Width of Tablecloth}}{\text{Fabric Width Minus Selvages and 1¼" (3.2cm) for Seams}} = \begin{array}{c}\text{Number of}\\\text{Panels}\\\text{Needed}\end{array}$$

3. Determine the total length of the tablecloth by adding twice the drop to the length or diameter of the table, then add 1¼" (3.2cm) for narrow hems or seam allowances for adding trims. If bias binding is used as a finish, no hem or seam allowance is required.

Length or Diameter of Table _____

+ Twice the Drop _____

+ 1¼" (3.2cm) for Hem or
Seam Allowance, if Required _____

_ _ _ _ _ _ _ _

Total Length of Tablecloth _____

4. Multiply the total length of the tablecloth times the number of panels needed to determine the basic fabric estimate. If working with plaids, stripes, or large prints which must be matched at the seams, add the length of one design repeat per panel to the fabric estimate. Divide by 36 (100) to convert this number into yards (meters).

$$\begin{array}{c}\text{Total Length} \\ \text{of Tablecloth}\end{array} \times \text{Number of Panels} = \begin{array}{c}\text{Basic} \\ \text{Fabric} \\ \text{Estimate}\end{array}$$

Basic Round Tablecloth with Bias Binding If preferred, you can use a narrow hem to finish the edge of a round tablecloth, omitting the bias binding suggested here.

HOW-TO

1. *Measure the table and estimate the fabric required (see page 179). To estimate how much double-fold bias binding to purchase, multiply the total width (diameter) by 3.25.*

2. *Test the fabric for shrinkage and straighten the grain (see* CUTTING FABRIC*).*

3. *If you need just one panel of fabric, use a yardstick (meterstick) to mark the cutting lines for the total width and total length of the tablecloth. Don't include the selvages.*

If you need more than one panel, plan to cut at least three—one full fabric-width central panel, and two equal partial fabric-width panels for the sides. This creates a balanced look, and avoids a seam at the center of the tablecloth. As you mark the cutting lines, don't include the selvages but remember to allow ⅝" (15mm) seam allowances. Match plaids, stripes, and large prints at the seams, and cut fabric with a one-way texture, sheen, or design using a with-nap cutting plan (see CUTTING FABRIC*).*

4. *If it's necessary to piece the panels, use French seams on sheers and ravel-prone fabrics. On other fabrics, use plain seams, press them open, and finish the raw edges (see* SEAMS*).*

5. *Fold the fabric into quarters to find the center (A). Pin to prevent shifting. Use a yardstick (meterstick) or a steel tape to measure the radius (half the total width of the cloth from the center), marking a curved cutting line from corner to corner (B).*

Cut each of the four fabric layers on this line (C), and unfold the fabric.

6. *Finish the edge by encasing it in bias binding (see* BIAS TAPES AND BINDINGS*).*

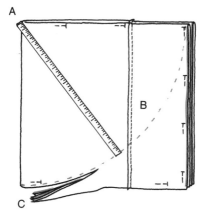

Round Tablecloth with Shirred Welting One easy way to enhance a basic round tablecloth is by adding a trim to the hemline.

Welting, shirred here as a custom detail, is a perfect choice, for it adds body and shape to the edge.

HOW-TO

1. *Measure the table and estimate the fabric required (see page 179). To determine how much* ³/₄" *(20mm) piping cord to buy for the welting, multiply the total width by 3.25. Allow extra for cutting fabric strips to cover the welting; use the "Estimating Bias Yield Chart" (see page 35) to determine how much extra fabric to allow.*

2. *Test the fabric for shrinkage and straighten the grain (see* CUTTING FABRIC*).*

3. *Follow steps 3 through 5 for the basic round tablecloth (see page 181).*

4. *Cut enough 3½" (9cm) wide crosswise strips to equal twice the length of the piping cord. Join the strips into one long strip, and use it to make shirred welting (see* WELTING*).*

5. *Pin the shirred welting to the right side of the tablecloth. Use a zipper foot to stitch in place (A), leaving the ends of the welting unstitched for about 2" (5cm).*

To join the ends, pull out the piping cord and trim the cord ends so they butt. Insert a pin about ¼" (6mm) from the cord ends to hold the shirred welting in place. Pull the threads out as far as the pin and tie in a knot. Trim the fabric so one raw edge can be turned under ¼" (6mm) and lapped over the other raw edge (B). Stitch the joined ends to the tablecloth.

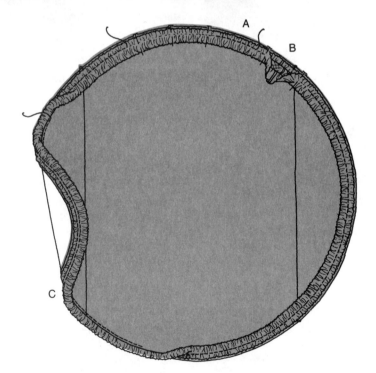

6. *Turn the welting down, and the seam allowances up toward the wrong side of the tablecloth. Steam, holding iron above table-* *cloth. From the right side, stitch next to the welting, through all thicknesses, to hold the welting seam allowance in place (C).*

182

Round Tablecloth with Ruffle
Use a fine, lightweight fabric such as batiste for this table-cloth so the ruffled edging will drape gracefully.

Turn under the remaining long edge ⅝" (15mm); press.

5. *Use pins to divide the ruffle and the tablecloth edge into 8 equal parts. Make two rows of long machine stitches ¼" (6mm) and ½" (13mm) from the edge between each pin-marked section (A). Matching the pin marks, pin the ruffle to the tablecloth, with the* wrong side *of the ruffle facing the* right side *of the tablecloth, having raw edges even. Gather the ruffle to fit the tablecloth (B).*

Stitch along both rows of gathering stitches (C).

HOW-TO

1. *Measure the table; subtract 6" (15cm) from the drop to allow for the extra length added by the ruffle and then estimate the fabric required (see page 180). To estimate how much fabric to add for the ruffle, multiply the total width of the tablecloth by 3.25, and use the estimating formulas for ruffles (see* RUFFLES*). The ruffle strips are cut 7¼" (18.5cm) wide.*

2. *Test the fabric for shrinkage and straighten the grain (see* CUTTING FABRIC*).*

3. *Follow steps 3 through 5 for the basic round tablecloth (see page 181).*

4. *Cut the ruffle strips. Join the strips with plain seams, pressed open, to make one continuous ruffle. Finish one long edge with a narrow hem (see* HEMS*).*

Tablecloth Extras

Here are some ideas for easy variations for tablecloths:

- Add body to decorative cloths by lining them to the edge. Use a beautiful fabric for the lining, and your cloth will be reversible.

- Quilt the fabric for a luxuriously draped full-length tablecloth.

- Scallop the edges, using a round template to draw the scallop stitching lines. Finish the edges with purchased or custom-made bias binding.

- Accent the shape of your table-cloth by stitching a band trim such as ribbon, braid, or galloon lace 2" to 4" (5 to 10cm) from the hem edge.

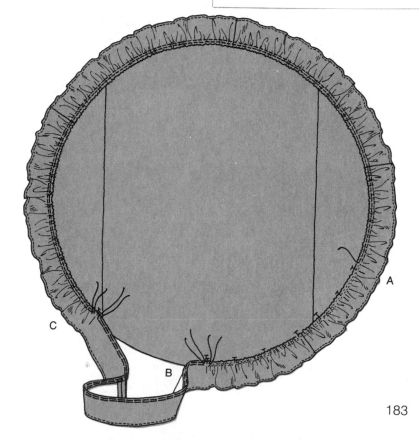

183

Basic Oval Tablecloth with Bias Binding If drawing an oval cutting line has always seemed difficult, this method shows you how to do it easily with a card-board template. If you prefer, you can use a narrow hem instead of purchased bias binding to finish the tablecloth edge.

HOW-TO

1. *Measure the table and estimate the fabric required (see page 179). To estimate how much double-fold bias binding to purchase, add the total length and width together, and multiply by 2.*

2. *Test the fabric for shrinkage and straighten the grain (see* CUTTING FABRIC).

3. *Follow steps 3 and 4 for the basic round tablecloth to cut and piece the fabric panels (see page 181).*

4. *To draw the oval cutting line, fold the fabric into quarters to find the center. Unfold the fabric and place the center of the fabric on the center of the tabletop. Use weights such as books to keep the fabric in position. Cut a strip of cardboard a little longer than the drop. Fold the cardboard so the distance from the edge of the strip to the fold equals the tablecloth drop. Place the fold on the edge of the tabletop to mark the cutting line around the fabric.*

Cut the fabric on the marked cutting line.

5. *Encase the raw edge with bias binding (see* BIAS TAPES AND BINDINGS).

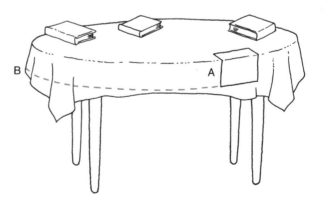

Basic Square or Rectangular Tablecloth with Bias Binding If you prefer, you can finish the edge of this tablecloth using a 2″ (5cm) deep plain hem with

mitered corners. Add 5″ (12.5cm) to the length and width of the tablecloth instead of 1¼″ (3.2cm) when estimating the fabric to allow for a deeper hem.

HOW-TO

1. *Measure the table and estimate the fabric required (see page 179). To estimate how much double-fold bias binding to purchase, add the total length and total width together, then multiply by 2; add at least 6″ (15cm) extra for mitering the corners and finishing the ends.*

2. *Test the fabric for shrinkage and straighten the grain (see* CUTTING FABRIC*).*

3. *Follow steps 3 and 4 for the basic round tablecloth to cut and piece the fabric panels (see page 181).*

4. *Encase the edge in bias binding, mitering the corners and finishing the ends (see* BIAS TAPES AND BINDINGS*).*

Square or Rectangular Tablecloth with Ruffle This romantically trimmed tablecloth is especially effective as the top cloth in a layered treatment.

Make the layers from matching or coordinating fabrics, or use lace for the top cloth, and a plain fabric underneath.

HOW-TO

1. *Measure the table; subtract 6″ (15cm) from the drop to allow for the extra length added by the ruffle and then estimate the fabric required (see page 180). To estimate how much fabric to add for the ruffle, calculate the length of the project edge by adding the total length and total width of the tablecloth together and multiplying by 2. Use the estimating formulas for ruffles (see* RUFFLES*); the ruffle strips are cut 7¼″ (18.5cm) wide.*

2. *Test the fabric for shrinkage and straighten the grain (see* CUTTING FABRIC*).*

3. *Follow steps 3 and 4 for the basic round tablecloth to cut and piece the fabric panels (see page 181).*

4. *Follow steps 4 and 5 for the round tablecloth with ruffle to make and apply the ruffle.*

Tabletop Accessories

NAPKINS

Cut a square of fabric and finish the edge—that's how to make a napkin. You can make your napkins any size you like, from 9½" (24cm) squares for cocktails, to the practical, lap-covering 18" to 20" (46 to 51cm) dinner size. Just remember to cut the napkin squares 1¼" (3.2cm) larger than the desired finished size if you want to finish the edge with a narrow hem (see HEMS). If you prefer to encase the edge in bias binding, cut the napkin to the finished size because no allowance is needed for the binding. (see BIAS TAPES AND BINDINGS).

To minimize fabric waste, consider how many napkins you can cut from a full width of fabric. If you use ⅝ yd (0.60m) of 45" (115cm) wide fabric, for example, you can cut two dinner-size napkins with few scraps left over. If you use ⅜ yd (0.35m) of 35" (90cm) wide fabric, you can cut three cocktail-size napkins with minimal fabric waste.

PLACEMATS

Placemats should be large enough to hold a single place setting—a standard size is 12" × 17" (30.5 × 43cm). Placemats can be used by themselves, or on top of a tablecloth for a layered look. Quilted fabric is ideal, but you could also use a double layer of fabric. If you like, place a layer of lightweight interfacing or thin batting between the two fabric layers to give the placemat body. Use two contrasting fabrics to make the placemats reversible, or use vinyl or synthetic suede for easy care.

Four standard placemats can be cut from about 1½ yds (1.40m) of 45" (115cm) wide quilted fabric. Buy twice as much fabric if you're cutting two layers of fabric for each placemat. Finish the edges with about 6½ yds (5.95m) of double-fold bias binding (see BIAS TAPES AND BINDINGS).

If you want to make placemats with a more formal feeling, cut them from linen, damask, or piqué, and use a satin stitch to finish the edges (see HEMS).

TABLE RUNNERS

Table runners are made like placemats, but they're cut much longer—the length or width of the table, plus a drop at each end. Make a single runner to dress a dining room table when it's not in use, or to cover a sideboard for a buffet. Or make several runners as alternatives to placemats—one runner for the length of the table, plus one or more to lay across the table as needed to make up place settings. A runner 13" × 72" (33 × 183cm) requires about 2⅛ yds (1.95m) of any width fabric, plus about 9 yds (8.25m) of bias binding; a 13" × 90" (33 × 229cm) runner requires about 2⅝ yds (2.40m) of any width fabric and 6 yds (5.50m) of bias binding.

RESOURCE DIRECTORY

This resource directory is a list of firms that manufacture or supply the items and services indicated. The prefix code letters, explained below, indicate the type of firm and what kind of inquiry should be directed to it for further information. In addition, check your local telephone directory for nearby suppliers of home furnishings items, which can often be purchased at retail. Also, fashion fabric stores nationwide are becoming increasingly good places to shop for home decorating fabrics and notions. Such traditionally apparel-oriented merchants may prove to be fruitful sources for your decorating needs.

Prefix Code Key

M **Manufacturer**—write for the name of the retail store nearest you. Manufacturers' showrooms are generally not open to the retail buying public.

S **Service supplier**—write for a price list and description of services available. Specify the type of service you desire.

R **Retailer**—write for a catalogue of merchandise available or visit.

Fabrics (FABRIC CODE KEY)

BATIKS, HANDCRAFTED PRIMITIVE
FABRICS . . . . **(BH)**

CASEMENTS, LACES, SHEERS . . . . **(S)**

LINING FABRICS . . . . **(L)**

PRINTED COTTONS, CHINTZES, SATEENS
. . . . **(PC)**

SOLID COTTONS, SYNTHETIC BLENDS
. . . . **(SC)**

SOLID AND NOVELTY WOVEN LINENS **(SL)**

UPHOLSTERY VELVETS, TAPESTRIES,
NOVELTY WOVENS, SATINS . . . . **(U)**

VINYL . . . . **(V)**

WALLCOVERING COORDINATED TO
FABRIC . . . . **(WC)**

M Anju–Woodridge Fabrics, Inc. . . . . . PC, SC, U, WC
295 Fifth Ave., New York, NY 10016
212–889–7000

M, R Laura Ashley, Inc. . . . . PC, WC
714 Madison Ave., New York, NY 10021
212–371–0606

M Barker Doral, Inc. . . . . S
261 Fifth Ave., New York, NY 10016
212–684–6022

M Bloomcraft . . . . PC, SC, S, U
295 Fifth Ave., New York, NY 10016
212–683–8900

M Cohama Riverdale . . . . PC, SC, U, WC
200 Madison Ave., New York, NY 10016
212–561–8500

M Covington Fabrics Corp. . . . . PC, SC, U
267 Fifth Ave., New York, NY 10016
212–689–2200

M Cyrus Clark Co., Inc. . . . . PC, SC
267 Fifth Ave., New York, NY 10016
212–684–5312

M Fabriyaz . . . . PC, SC, WC
41 Madison Ave., New York, NY 10010
212–686–3311

M Far Eastern Fabrics, Ltd. BH
171 Madison Ave., New York, NY 10016
212–683–2623

M Hamilton Adams Imports . . . . SL
104 West 40th St., New York, NY 10018
212–221–0800

M International Printworks, Inc. . . . . PC, V, WC
P.O. Box 479, Needham, MA 02192
617–449–6990

M P. Kaufmann . . . . PC, SC, WC
261 Fifth Ave., New York, NY 10016
212–686–6470

M Lace Country, Division of Emil Katz & Co., Inc. . . . S
21 West 38th St., New York, NY 10018
212–221–6171

R Pierre Deux Fabrics . . . . PC, WC
870 Madison Ave., New York, NY 10021
212–570–9343

M Rockland Mills L
261 Fifth Ave., New York, NY 10016
212–679–9220

M Spring Mills Retail and Specialty Fabric Division
. . . . PC, SC
1430 Broadway, New York, NY 10018
212–556–6579

M UniRoyal V
312 North Hill St., P.O. Box 2000, Mishawaka,
IN 46544
219–256–8292

M VIP Division of Cranston Printworks . . . . PC
1412 Broadway, New York, NY 10018
212–730–4600

M John Wolf Decorative Fabrics Division of Cone Mills
. . . . PC, SC
261 Fifth Ave., New York, NY 10016
212–398–1400

M Wolf–Gordon Vinyl Fabrics V
132 West 21st St., New York, NY 10010
212–255–3300

MAIL ORDER FABRICS

R Conrans . . . . PC, SC
145 Huguenot St., New Rochelle, NY 10801
914–632–0515

R Jensen Lewis . . . . SC
89 Seventh Ave., New York, NY 10011
212–929–4880

M, R Laura Ashley . . . . PC
714 Madison Ave., New York, NY 10021
212–371–0606

R Leiters . . . . PC, SC
Box 978, Kansas City, MO 64141
816–221–3100

Fabric Services
(FABRIC SERVICES CODE KEY)

BACKING FOR UPHOLSTERY,
WALLCOVERINGS . . . . **(BA)**
FLAMEPROOFING . . . . **(FP)**
LAMINATING . . . . **(LA)**
QUILTING . . . . **(Q)**
STAINPROOFING . . . . **(SP)**
VINYL COATING . . . . **(VC)**

S Custom Laminations, Inc. . . . . . . FP, LA, SP, VC, BA
P.O. Box 2066, 932 Market St., Paterson, NJ 07509
201–274–9174

S Decorative Quilting Co., Inc. . . . . Q
448 East 183rd St., Bronx, NY 10458
212–584–2216

S Dupont Zepel–Dyes Chemicals Division E.I.Dupont
De Nemours & Co. . . . . SP
350 Fifth Ave., Room 1116, New York, NY 10001
212–971–4781

S Fabric Quilters Unlimited, Inc. . . . . Q
1400 Shames Drive, Westbury, NY 11590
516–333–2866

S Fiber-Seal International, Inc. . . . . SP
11714 Forest Central Drive, Dallas, TX 75243
214–349–8374

S Guild Needlecraft, Inc. . . . . Q
119 West 23rd St., New York, NY 10011
212–989–8822

S   Kiesling Hess . . . . FP, SP, BA
1011 Wood St., Philadelphia, PA 19107
215–922–5686

S   New York Flameproofing Co., Inc. . . . . FP
60 West 18th St., New York, NY 10011
212–924–7200

S   Quiltco . . . . Q
112 Lincoln Ave., Bronx, NY 10454
212–292–9494

S   Quiltsmith . . . . Q
20 Winchester St., Brookline, MA 02146
617–277–3279

S   Scotchguard Protectors, 3M Company . . . . SP
3M Center, St. Paul, MN 55101
612–733–1110

Trimmings (TRIMMINGS CODE KEY) ▬▬

DECORATIVE BRAIDS . . . . (DB)

DECORATIVE FRINGE . . . . (DF)

LACE TRIMMINGS . . . . (LT)

RIBBONS . . . . (R)

M   C. M. Offray . . . . R
261 Madison Ave., New York NY 10016
212–682–8010

M   Conso Products Co. . . . . DB
261 Fifth Ave., New York, NY 10016
212–532–9060

M   Europa Imports Inc. . . . . DB
2330 Old Middlefield Wy #10, Mt. View, CA 94043
415–969–3232

M   Grayblock Ribbon Co., Inc. . . . . R
64 West 36th St., New York, NY 10018
212–947–7129

R   Hyman Hendler and Sons . . . . R
67 West 38th St., New York, NY 10018
212–840–8393

R   Tinsel Trading Co. . . . . DB, DF
47 West 38th St., New York, NY 10018
212–730–1030

M   Waverly Fabrics Division of F. Schumacher & Co.
. . . . DB
939 Third Ave., New York, NY 10022
212–644–5900

M   William E. Wright and Co. . . . . DB, DF, LT
1 Penn Plaza, New York, NY 10001
212–947–4866

Notions and Hardware
(PILLOWS, QUILTS CODE KEY) ▬▬

BATTING . . . . (B)

CUSHION FILLING MATERIALS . . . . (CM)

DOWN AND FEATHERS . . . . (DO)

FOAM . . . . (F)

PILLOW FORMS AND BOLSTERS . . . . . (PF)

CLOSURES . . . . (C)

R   Comfort Industries . . . . PF, F
35-39 21st St., Long Island City, NY 11101
718–389–0900

R   Dixie Foam . . . . F
20 East 20th St., New York, NY 10003
212–777–3626

M   Fairfield Processing Corp. . . . . B, PF, CM
88 Rose Hill Ave., Danbury, CT 06810
800–243–0989

R   Greentex Upholstery Supplies . . . . CM, B, C, F
244 East 58th St., New York, NY 10022
212–755–7166

R   Itzkowitz . . . . DO, PF
161 Allen St., New York, NY 10002
212–477–1788

M   Stearns & Foster Co. . . . . B, CM, PF
117 Williams St., Cincinnati, OH 45215
513–948–5296

R   York Feather and Down . . . . DO
10 Evergreen Ave., Brooklyn, NY 11206
718–497–4120

M   Velcro Corporation C
681 Fifth Ave., New York, NY 10022
212–751–2144

Notions and Hardware (WINDOWS, DECORATIVE, MISCELLANEOUS CODE KEY) ∎

DECORATIVE HARDWARE . . . . **D**

DRAPERY HOOKS, RODS . . . . **HR**

LAMPSHADE FRAMES . . . . **LF**

SHADE TAPES, HARDWARE . . . . **SH**

UPHOLSTERY SUPPLIES . . . . **US**

M   Graber Industries . . . . HR, SH, D
Graber Plaza, Middleton, WI 53562
608–836–1011

R   Greentex Upholstery Supplies . . . . HR, SH, US
244 East 58th St., New York, NY 10022
212–755–7166

M   Kirsch . . . . HR, D
261 Fifth Ave., New York, NY 10016
212–651–2311

M   Master Recessed Systems, Inc. . . . . HR
1800 New Highway, Farmingdale, NY 11735
516–822–5310

R   P. E. Guerin, Inc. . . . . D
23 Jane St., New York, NY 10014
212–243–5270

R   Salmagundi Farms, Ltd. . . . . LF
P.O. Box 789, Coopville, WA 98239
206–678–5888

R   Van Wyck Drapery Hardware Supply Corp. . . . . HR,
SH, US
39 Eldridge St., New York, NY 11203
212–925–1300